STRAITJACKET SOCIETY

STRAITJACKET SOCIETY

An Insider's Irreverent View of Bureaucratic Japan

MASAO MIYAMOTO, M.D.
FOREWORD BY Juzo Itami

KODANSHA INTERNATIONAL
Tokyo • New York • London

The publisher wishes to thank Juliet Winters Carpenter and Eric Gower for
their assistance with this volume. For their translation work on Mr. Itami's
piece, the publisher gratefully acknowledges S & G Japan, Inc.

Published in Japanese by Kodansha as Oyakusho no Okite.

Distributed in the United States by Kodansha America, Inc.,
114 Fifth Avenue, New York, New York 10011, and in the United Kingdom
and continental Europe by Kodansha Europe Ltd., 95 Aldwych, London
WC2B 4JF.

Published by Kodansha International Ltd., 17–14 Otowa 1-chome,
Bunkyo-ku, Tokyo 112, and Kodansha America, Inc.

LIBRARY OF CONGRESS CATALOGUING-IN-PUBLICATION DATA
Miyamoto, Masao, 1948–
[Oyakusho no okite. English]
Straitjacket society / by Masao Miyamoto: introduction by Juzo Itami;
translated by Juliet Winters Carpenter.
1. Civil service ethics–Japan. 2. Japan–Officials and employees–Conduct of
life. 3. Bureaucracy–Japan. 4. Miyamoto, Masao, 1948– . I. Title.
JQ1629. E8M6913 1996 306'.0952–dc20 94–11563 CIP

ISBN 4–7700–1848–7

To Lori

Contents

Foreword

THIS BOOK provides an inside glimpse of Japan's notorious bureaucracy from the eyes of a psychiatrist-turned-bureaucrat. The modifier "notorious" will, no doubt, offend some people. There's actually a wide range of opinions, from the laudatory to the disparaging, on the Japanese bureaucracy. A short recap of the history behind this institution will, I think, help non-Japanese readers appreciate the poignancy of Dr. Miyamoto's sketches of life within the bureaucracy.

In 1854, American ships under the command of Commodore Matthew Perry sailed into Tokyo Bay and forced Japan to open itself to trade. By then the Great Powers had already divided most of the world into spheres of influence. Japan, which had existed in self-imposed isolation for nearly three hundred years, was thrown into social and political upheaval. The new leaders who led the overthrow of the feudal system fourteen years later felt compelled to catch up quickly. Rapid modernization followed in the wake of the revolution, along with the adoption of a constitution, a national legal system, a version of parliamentary democracy, and other elements of the modern nation state, all modeled more or less along Western lines. The Emperor became a constitutional monarch.

Japan's ultimate goal was economic and military equality with the Great Powers. To achieve this national goal in the shortest amount of time, an elite group of proto-bureaucrats—mostly

9

former samurai who came to dominate the government—took it upon themselves to force a then relatively ignorant citizenry in the desired direction. All human, natural, and other resources were mobilized to realize the grand national design envisioned by these bureaucrats.

In this rush for parity with the Great Powers, the bureaucrats accumulated tremendous power. Their control was accepted by the people, who, having just emerged from feudalism, had no experience with anything other than hierarchical rule. In short, the new bureaucrats replaced the daimyo fief-holders and samurai retainers, who, as their role of warrior declined, had come to exercise most local administrative duties at the apex of political power.

From the start, the Japanese bureaucracy was based on the premise that the citizenry was ignorant and needed leaders, and since parlimentarians were chosen by an ignorant electorate they too were ignorant. Under this assumption, the bureaucrats felt it was natural and proper that they become the de facto national leaders. Today, in 1994, these assumptions remain unchanged.

Under this arrangement, Japan almost became a Great Power itself before losing everything in the disaster of World War II. During those cataclysmic years, the bureaucrats invaded every conceivable area of people's lives, justifying their actions as wartime necessities. The powers nominally vested in the Diet and in political parties evaporated, as the "Emperor's bureaucrats" assumed virtually dictatorial control.

From the ashes of defeat, Japan was remodeled, more or less, into an American-style democracy at the fiat of the United States. A new constitution was written by the Americans, providing for a separation of power among the executive, legislative, and judicial branches of government. The constitution also granted far more autonomy to local jurisdictions.

In the American-written constitution, the popularly elected Diet was to be the sole repository of legislative power. Naturally, this blueprint of where power would legally reside presented the ultimate crisis for the bureaucrats: the new constitution was about to effectively deprive them of their control of the reins of the Japanese legislative process.

To circumvent the intent, if not the letter, of the constitution—which explicitly forbids bureaucrats from taking part in the legislative process—the bureaucrats sneaked through a clause in the Cabinet Act that allowed them to propose bills. They then added a similar clause to the Diet Act, permitting them to join Diet deliberations of their own proposals as formal members of the various committees.

Almost by default, elected representatives—few of whom had any specialized expertise in the legislative process itself—left the actual drafting of bills to the bureaucrats. Diet debate became a mere formality. Cabinet ministers and Diet members literally read to each other from scripts authored by the same bureaucrats. In the end, the bureaucracy reemerged as the dominant force behind Japan's legislative process.

Local autonomy suffered a similar fate. The bureaucrats needed powerful centralized control to realize their aims. An American-style division of states, each with its own independent legislative, executive, and other institutions like a local militia, police, and courts, was their worst nightmare.

Acting counter to American occupation policy, the bureaucrats first manipulated to bring governors under the central government's control. Officially, governors were still elected locally, as spelled out by the Americans, but since their jobs had both local and national implications, the bureaucrats made a case that "uncooperative governors" could hinder national efforts. Once this claim was accepted, the central government gained the power to issue directives to locally elected governors and press for their implementation. Power was also given, *in extremis,* to dismiss local governors. As a result, local governors became the minions of the national bureaucrats.

According to the original American design, local governments were to be granted the power to enact their own laws and ordinances. To jump this troublesome hurdle, the bureaucrats added a convenient provision: by appending the words ". . . unless otherwise stipulated by national law or government directives based thereupon," they effectively gutted the clause. It was left to the national government to decide what might be "otherwise stipulated."

Under occupation guidelines, local governments were to take the first share of all tax revenues, leaving the surplus for the central government. The bureaucrats cunningly negated this policy by saying that such critical national undertakings as foreign affairs, defense, and nationwide infrastructure projects should receive priority funding. The Americans accepted this argument, and the bureaucrats emerged triumphant once again. It was left to them to decide what tax-funded undertakings would be "national" in scope. Under their subsequent interpretations, even the development of local rail facilities and their environs became a national project since they could be considered part of the nationwide urban development scheme.

By assuming virtually total control over tax revenues, the central government began allocating funds for local undertakings, a power they have wielded condescendingly over the years. Today prefectural governors and city mayors spend most of their time in various bureaucratic offices begging for subsidies. In effect, local governments became nothing more than branch offices of the central bureaucracy.

The democratic separation of powers and decentralization of authority guaranteed in Japan's constitution exist today in name only. Despite the best intentions of the United States to

democratize Japan immediately after the war, Japanese bureaucrats were able to retain their traditional and primary role, first
established in the Meiji era (1868–1912): to protect and foster
industrial growth. The bureaucracy has always believed that
state capitalism (that is, bureaucratically guided economic
policies) was the most effective way for a developing country to
catch up. Japan's postwar economic miracle seems to have
proven them right.

In this particular sense, Japanese bureaucrats have done
very well. Through tight regulatory activities, they nurtured
industry, created millions of jobs, lifted Japan's standard of living, and closed the gap between the former haves and have-nots
in a way that even a Fabian socialist could only envy. There are
some deep-rooted problems, however, with this kind of economic system. Admittedly, bureaucratic intervention is effective in protecting and fostering industrial growth that allows
developing nations to close the gap between themselves and
more developed economies. That is to say, the model works
beautifully as long the goal is to "catch up." But in the case of
Japan, which has more than caught up and now finds itself in a
position to lead a global economy based on free trade and competition, these same bureaucratic techniques are no longer
valid. The bureaucracy's biggest problem is that its policies
have become obsolete.

Japan is no longer "catching up." It no longer models itself
on what it once perceived as more advanced nations. Today,
Japan must develop new, globally competitive technologies,
products and services. Bureaucrats, however, are only good at
harnessing the national vitality under a system of state capitalism or socialism. It is becoming more and more apparent that
they are not capable of inspiring human or social creativity.
In fact, they are most often counterproductive when dealing
with matters of the spirit.

As preservers instead of creators, bureaucrats tend to

provide assistance to lagging industries. This hampers natural competition in the private sector and perpetuates uncompetitive, obsolete industries and business practices, slows down a society's metabolism, and obstructs its spontaneous and natural urge toward ever higher creativity and efficiency.

For more than a century, Japan's bureaucracy-driven government has created grossly inflated roles for bureaucrats. People's activities are tightly hedged by a countless number of government rules and regulations, depriving society of its natural flexibility.

The gigantic bureaucratic system has become self-perpetuating. As a result, the bureaucracy is now less of a functional necessity and more of an inbred, *Gemeinschaft*-like community. As for the bureaucrats themselves, their primary purposes are belonging to that community, maintaining harmony within it, and perpetuating its existence as long as possible. Those daring enough to try something new are distrusted. The most respected are those who avoid change and scrupulously avoid making mistakes that might upset the status quo.

The source of all bureaucratic power is authority, based on government regulations, to give or withhold permission. Bureaucrats relentlessly endeavor to maintain and expand this authority by constantly devising new regulations, rules, and policies that will bring more power in their hands. At the same time, they will never willingly relinquish older sources of power, no matter how obsolete or detrimental to society's greater good.

For the average Japanese person such as myself, the greatest problem concerning the bureaucracy is that it has usurped so much legislative power. Unlike politicians, bureaucrats cannot be voted out of office. We may be unhappy about the bureaucrats, but we have no way of registering our dissatisfaction. In short, we are powerless to influence this most important of all Japanese institutions, no matter how poorly it serves us.

It is of course unrealistic to expect the bureaucrats to reform from within. The bureaucratic system has grown so enormous that, in many ways, it *is* Japan itself. We must also remember that preservation of the bureaucratic system has become the raison d'être of the bureaucrats themselves. It is also unrealistic to expect elected politicians to take the lead; they would have to depend on the bureaucracy itself to write the initial reform legislation.

All of this notwithstanding, we cannot abandon hope. Fortunately, there are a handful of conscientious Japanese bureaucrats who are truly concerned about the current circumstances clouding Japan's future. They are seriously trying to find ways to reform the system.

It is not likely that they will succeed without help. Only when their passion for reform is supported by public opinion and outsiders—intellectuals, businessmen, journalists, citizens' groups, conscientious politicians, and local bureaucrats—can we expect anything to happen. We should also consider the importance of international opinion, to which Japanese are becoming acutely sensitive. As long as the bureaucrats continue to protect certain industries and insist on the maintenance of various peculiar business practices which impede free and fair competition, it seems likely that international criticism will increase. External pressure can also help trigger reform.

At any rate, we on the outside cannot but hope that more insiders, like the author of this book, will have the courage to call for reform.

Dr. Miyamoto studied psychoanalysis in the United States, practiced psychiatry for several years there, and returned to Japan to become a bureaucrat. It is fascinating to note how his pre-bureaucrat values, acquired through his unique career and in many ways influenced by American values, have given him an objectivity rare among his colleagues.

The contradictions and problems of any society often seem

so natural to its individual members they are accepted as a matter of course—the conundrum of the forest and the trees. Most Japanese accept the bureaucracy as being as natural to their country as cherry blossoms. But, as the author shows, it is the source of many of today's problems.

"O wad some power the giftie gie us, to see ourselves as others see us" is as true for nations as it is for individuals. The author's message is a fascinating manifestation of that old adage.

Juzo Itami
May 1994

Introduction

IN JAPAN, bureaucratic positions are highly respected because everyone knows that bureaucrats wield enormous power. Thus, when most Japanese hear that I am the director of quarantine at the Port of Kobe, they usually remark, "That sounds like a wonderful job." In reality, the position of director of quarantine for the Ministry of Health and Welfare is a dead-end job, so I always reveal the truth to them. What strikes me is that when I tell them what it's really like, most people look shocked. In Japan, unless you have a close relationship, it is unthinkable to speak so frankly. People are more comfortable exchanging ritualistic pleasantries, and scrupulously avoid anything that might cause discomfort or shock. A tacit agreement exists not to reveal one's true feelings or situation.

When I was first assigned to the quarantine division at the Port of Tokyo, I complained to my superior at the ministry's headquarters that I had nothing to do and was bored. He answered, "Just sit at your desk from nine to five. You are not being asked to do anything. Remember, you are there to shape up, to reflect on your past. Try reading some books." So that is what I did. However, as it turns out, all of that reading actually helped to sharpen the sword I now use in fighting the bureaucracy.

How did I end up in these circumstances? Having lived in the United States for ten years, where I worked in the field of psychiatry and psychoanalysis in New York City, I developed a professional capacity to look at things objectively, particularly in the field of human relationships. I also learned to assert myself. When you get used to this way of communication, it is difficult to change, because the desire to express and assert oneself is natural.

My first year in America was very difficult. I did not have a good grasp of English, but people were generally very helpful, frequently offering me directions and advice. However, compared to my first year in America, returning to Japan was onerous. Despite the fact that I was returning to my home country, I encountered nothing but problems. Ten years of absence created a gap in my knowledge and behavior which my colleagues did not appreciate. They taunted me continually, and I was soon psychologically drained.

Straitjacket Society is a translation of *Oyakusho no Okite*, which was published in April 1993 when I was the director of quarantine for the Port of Yokohama, a much larger city than Kobe. The original title literally means "code of the bureaucrats." *Oyakusho no Okite* was a compilation of the articles about my experiences which ran in a monthly magazine published by the *Asahi Shimbun*, the Japanese equivalent of the *New York Times*. When I wrote these articles in May–December 1992, I was the director of quarantine for the Port of Tokyo, my first demotion.

The bureaucracy's response to the impact this book has had is curious. The more controversial I become, the more the public responds; the greater the public response, the farther I am removed from Tokyo. My position in the quarantine section is more than a little ironic—I am literally being quarantined from the political and economic center of Japan. By the time this book is published in English, there is no telling where I will be posted.

I must confess that I was astonished when *Oyakusho no Okite* became a bestseller. What I essentially said in the book was that I wanted respect for my private life. I described how difficult it was to take a vacation of two or more consecutive weeks; my unwillingness to participate in unpaid overtime; how I did not want to be told what style and color my clothes should be; and my reluctance to be stuck with my colleagues day and night, seven days a week, like most other bureaucrats. I am certain that the problems I raise in this book are not controversial in other developed countries. But in Japan, particularly in the close-minded bureaucracy, when you reveal these things, you are labeled a nemesis, a heretic, a renegade.

Since this book was published in Japanese, I have been bombarded with requests for interviews from both the Japanese and foreign mass media. It is hard for people outside Japan to believe that a two-week vacation in the south of France would create an uproar. This incident, detailed in chapter four, tells something about Japanese society, which is why foreign correspondents were curious about what I had to say. On the surface, Japanese bureaucrats tell Western countries that Japan is the same as any other advanced country, but in reality there are many differences. One of these differences can be seen in the way Japanese and foreign journalists interviewed me. The Western correspondents were confrontational, at times playing devil's advocate to stimulate the interview. The Japanese correspondents, on the other hand, asked questions, and then silently recorded my response.

It was surprising enough to be interviewed by foreign correspondents, but I was flabbergasted when I received a call from the American embassy informing me that Ambassador Mondale wanted to invite me for lunch. I subsequently received invitations from a visiting state department official, diplomats of the French and Italian governments, and requests to lecture at foreign chambers of commerce in Japan. I was puzzled as to why these people would be interested in me, a person who holds a dead-end position in the Japanese government. The answer, I later realized, was that it is highly unusual for someone to reveal heretofore unspoken truths about life inside the government. What they wanted was insight into the Japanese bureaucracy.

The following points crystallize some of the major aspects of the Japanese bureaucracy, the ultimate microcosm of Japanese society.

* The bureaucracy is the biggest trade barrier to entry into the Japanese market, since the bureaucracy controls the entire market through a system of regulations and permits. If the market were truly open, it would enrich the lives of consumers in both Japan and the West. But this would mean downsizing and restructuring, to which the bureaucrats would never agree. Therefore, do not expect any meaningful deregulation in the future.

* The interests of producers are consistently given priority over those of consumers because the bureaucrats see the enlargement of Japan Inc., as their overriding goal.

* To expand Japan Inc., the bureaucracy introduced the philosophy of *messhi hoko*, or self-sacrifice for the sake of the group. This philosophy requires the subordination of individual lives to the good of the whole. Since all Japanese invariably belong to some sort of group, through this philosophy they end up sacrificing their personal lives, voluntarily or otherwise.

It is difficult to say no to *messhi hoko* and look for another job, since most Japanese companies are based on this philosophy. A person who rejects the concept of self-sacrifice can expect total isolation from the group. The fear of ostracism evokes strong anxiety in most Japanese, therefore the threat of removal from the group exerts a strong controlling influence on individual behavior.

* In psychological terms, the stimulation of masochistic tendencies equals pleasure. The more you lose your personal life, the more pleasure you get, and as it is very difficult to resist the centripetal force of *messhi hoko*, this philosophy has become a very efficient way to control people. It has infiltrated the daily lives of the Japanese, particularly through the education system, which the bureaucrats of course control.

* The Japanese are educated so that even if they are frustrated or unhappy, they will resign themselves to the situation. This education is very important since, if people do not complain, it is easier to propagate the philosophy of *messhi hoko*.

* To accomplish the goal that every Japanese embrace the philosophy of *messhi hoko*, the bureaucrats introduced an educational program based on the idea that all Japanese should look, think, and act alike. This type of education does not allow for individual differences, and as a result, creativity is severely curtailed. From a psychiatrist's point of view, the bureaucrats are asking people to embrace an illusion.

* Ultimately the bureaucracy does not want people to be independent. Being independent means that a person expresses his thoughts openly, develops a capacity to say no, and questions the status quo. *Messhi hoko* prevents people from becoming independent. What this means in terms of personality structure is that a person's pride is

fragile, and he can be easily injured. However, a greater problem with the inability to develop independence is the concomitant lack of impulse control. This is the main reason why Japanese cannot say no. What *messhi hoko* does is to arrest development at the stage of adolescence.

* Envy is a hostile impulse. In the West, the feeling of envy is condemned, but in Japan envy is condoned as a form of justice. If envy is sanctioned, it is difficult to develop one's talent. Creativity by definition stands out, and in Japan, since any deviation from the group elicits a hostile response, talented people become victims. When viewed from this perspective, Japan resembles a socialist or even a communist country, where idealism develops to prevent envy from arising among the people.

When independence is discouraged and envy is socially accepted, the Japanese people have no choice but to depend on bureaucrats, who function metaphorically as a mother figure. The bureaucrats take advantage of this inability to develop independence in order to maintain control of Japan Inc. One could say that Japanese bureaucrats, in addition to controlling the economy and politics, also control the maturation of human development.

* The bureaucrats announce to the world that Japan is a democracy with a free-market economy. But Japanese society functions like a totalitarian country because, even though the separation of the three branches of government is constitutionally guaranteed, bureaucratic control of all forms of power is nearly absolute. Once you belong to a group, freedom of expression disappears. Open expression of critical thoughts is not tolerated without approval by the entire group. In addition, the regulatory

power the bureaucracy wields over the economy curtails consumers' freedom of choice.

What distinguishes Japan's "totalitarianism" is that there is no observable Big Brother figure. It is the structure itself that functions as Big Brother. This kind of structure makes it almost impossible to change the system.

This book takes a very critical look at the bureaucracy. However, I would like readers to know that there are many bureaucrats who find this structure to be a major problem. But due to the very structure, no change will occur unless bureaucrats are willing to jeopardize their careers. As I pointed out earlier, a horizontal move in Japanese society is very difficult, and no one inside the system, up until now, has voiced open criticism.

It is very sad for me to see that, despite the overwhelmingly positive response to this book from the Japanese public, as well as from foreign political and business leaders, the Ministry of Health and Welfare cannot look at the situation objectively. The ministry relentlessly keeps pushing me further and further away from any meaningful position.

Recently I spoke with a professor who was formerly employed by the Ministry of Health and Welfare. He told me, "These days many people in the ministry are beginning to acknowledge your comments. But once the system has made a decision, it is impossible to reverse it. So you should be aware that there is no chance of you being returned to Tokyo. Even if a majority of people in the ministry want you to return to Tokyo, once a policy has been initiated it can't be changed."

He continued, "It's a lot like Japan's involvement in World War Two. When the invasion of Asia started, many people thought that it was the wrong step for Japan to take, yet no one was able to stop the tragic course of events. It was only the devastating impact of the atomic bomb that put an end to

Imperial Japan." He then half-jokingly said, "So there is a small chance for you to be returned to Tokyo, if foreign pressure is applied on your behalf."

According to someone close to the power center of the ministry, I have no chance for further promotion. So why don't I quit? This question is often raised, and the answer is that I have discovered a weak spot in the system. The bureaucracy has an extremely hard outer shell, which is impervious to external pressure and criticism. No matter how many people on the outside call for change, it will have little effect. But as powerful as this outer shell is, there is a more fragile shell underneath. The assumption that no one inside the group will be openly critical or transgress the code of the group renders inside criticism a viable force for change.

Since the system is based on illusion, pointing out reality brings about disillusionment, and disillusionment causes cracks in the system. Most Japanese find themselves to be powerless against the bureaucracy, but they should be aware that they have the power to change the system.

Instead of valuing the masochistic pleasure of *messhi hoko*, if the Japanese focus on the pleasure of freedom, they can hatch from their adolescent shells and become independent adults. Freed from the constraints of the bureaucracy, they will then be able to lead richer, more meaningful lives.

July 4, 1994

Straitjacket Society

Rules for Aspiring Bureaucrats

The Almighty Diet

"Your timing couldn't have been better," my supervisor beamed. "It's a stroke of luck for you to join the ministry just when we're about to revise the Mental Health Law. There's no higher honor for a government official than to be involved in legal revisions."

The year was 1986. I had just returned to Japan after an extended stay in the United States, joining the Ministry of Health and Welfare as deputy director of the Mental Health Division of the Public Health Department. My erstwhile supervisor welcomed me with the above words.

To me, however, his comment was unsettling. I had joined the ministry to execute laws, not make them. I couldn't yet grasp the connection in Japan between the executive and legislative branches of government. Accustomed to American-style separation of powers, I could only wonder why a government administrator like myself would be drafting bills—surely that was the job of the legislators!

Still, I was game for anything, and I gave the drafting of the bill my best shot.

In the process, what struck me was the unbelievable importance bureaucrats attached to Diet testimony. "Representative So-and-so has begun his questioning," someone would say. Whenever the Diet was in session, play-by-play accounts of the proceedings were broadcast over the Health Ministry's PA system. Should the Standing Committee on the Budget happen to be involved, moreover, continuous live coverage was shown on our section's television. Such practices, in themselves, created the overpowering impression that the Diet must be a very important place indeed. I remember that, as a newcomer, I kept my eyes glued to the screen.

The Diet has absolute sway over every member of the government bureaucracy. For a bureaucrat, the rhythm of daily life itself hinges on the Diet. As long as the Diet is in session, no one is allowed to go home at night until the next day's questions are known. This is known as "Diet standby." Standby alerts are issued by the general affairs department, but if the deputy director in charge is excessively cautious, more sections than necessary may receive orders to stay on. "Voluntary over-time" is the charming euphemism employed to describe our all-nighters.

As a way of dealing with Diet standby, reception rooms of the central government are transformed into saloons after six. Everybody hangs around waiting for the standby to be lifted, killing time by drinking beer and listening idly as people go on grumbling about the powers that be, or keeping one eye on the dull television fare as they slurp down noodles that have sat too long.

For some reason, bureaucrats respond to Diet members with unconditional obedience. Requests for materials cause general pandemonium, disrupting normal operations entirely. Such an exaggerated response to a request from the head of one's own ministry might be understandable, but to be thrown into a tizzy by a request for information from a *zoku giin* (a member of a "tribe" or "family" within a political party that focuses on specific sectors) makes little sense.

Still, bureaucrats have their canny side, and in fact the level of response varies according to the party of the politician in question. A representative of the Liberal Democratic Party (LDP), for example, who might have sway over office personnel decisions, receives an extraordinarily thorough reply, with page after page of extra information that no one is ever likely to read. At the opposite extreme is the Japan Communist Party (JCP), which gets no more information than the average person could obtain with a minimum of effort.

Generally, though, the level of response, even to the Communist party, seems more than adequate. Moreover, the administrative structure shouldn't function as the private secretarial organization of the party in power. If politicians need materials, they ought to use their own brainpower and resources to get them and not rely on the administrative structure at every turn.

Sutra-chanting and Question-gathering

Three months after I joined the ministry, my section chief realized that I had never been to the Diet. "Go listen to the parliamentary interpellations," I was told. "The experience will serve you well."

I set off in a state of considerable excitement for my first trip to the Diet. To my surprise, I found that even a new employee like myself was able to take the official limousine to the Diet. Inside, every time you pass through security, you are saluted by police officers and guards, giving rise to the pleasant illusion that you are some sort of VIP. It's not hard to see why people become addicted to the sensation.

Every government agency has its own waiting room inside the Diet, and I was ushered into the room designated for Ministry of Health and Welfare officials. After registering there, I was handed a badge giving me free passage into both the Upper and Lower Houses. It was tied with string to my registration card, which served as ID. I was instructed to place the registration card in my breastpocket and wear the badge on my suit lapel. I did so, only to have my director advise me, "Miyamoto, let your badge dangle down on your chest." The director general was right next to me, so I looked to see what he had done with his badge. It was pinned neatly to his lapel. Then I understood. Government hierarchy resembles the military. A relative nobody like me was not to be too self-assertive.

Finally, I entered the committee room where the question-and-answer session was taking place. Eminent men representing the populace were hurling difficult questions at bureaucrats said to represent the highest level of Japanese brainpower. And yet, the more I listened, the more I inclined to yawn. There was no sense of tension whatsoever. It was like listening to a Buddhist priest chant a sutra in characteristic singsong style. (In fact, insiders' slang for a briefing session on a new piece of legislation is *okyo-yomi*, "sutra-chanting," so my impression was not far off the mark.)

The boredom was overwhelming. To gain some relief, I tried playing a game of association. My first association was of an uninspired professor reading lecture notes aloud as students furiously took down his every word. Tiring of that game, I found myself surrounded by pleasant angels of sleep who graciously transformed the deadly-dull sutra into a soft lullaby. The lure of angelic voices is not easy for me to resist. I must have dozed off for about five minutes. Then suddenly, someone gave me a poke in the ribs. Opening my eyes as if in a dream, I discovered the culprit to be the director of legal affairs. He seemed determined to wake me from my slumber. I ignored the pest and went on with my comfortable siesta, whereupon he ordered me in all seriousness to take notes.

As I had never been to the Diet before, this seemed to me a reasonable request. I scrambled up, rubbed the sleep out of my eyes, and tried to take notes. It couldn't be done: even when I could understand the point of the questions, the answers seemed so circular and evasive that I had trouble writing down their gist. The session ended with some trepidation on my part.

Back at the Ministry of Health and Welfare, I came under concerted attack for having fallen asleep at my first Diet session. I tried to defend myself by pointing out that Diet members had been sleeping, too, only to be scolded again: "You're certainly no Diet member. Remember your place." The only bright spot was the director, who laughed and forgave my transgression. But from then on, I was known by the unwelcome nickname of "Sleepy Miyamoto."

When I had grown more accustomed to life in the government offices, I received an order to go "question-gathering." This is another peculiar chore that comes with the job. It involves going to the Diet chambers to receive copies of questions a Diet member plans to ask the following day.

"Separation of Powers": Myth and Reality

The Diet is known as a center of discussion; I had always thought of it as a place where members representing the people debated their views and worked them into the form of binding legislation. In the United States, where the separation of powers is absolute, someone from the administration might be summoned to testify before Congress, but could never take center stage in a Congressional debate. Even in countries with a parliamentary system like that of Japan, such as the United Kingdom, the boundary between the executive and legislative branches is clear.

Before returning to Japan, I had blithely supposed that the system of tripartite separation of powers was established under the constitution in Japan as well. It didn't take long to realize, however, that there was a discrepancy between the official line on separation of powers and the way things are actually done.

One evening at a dinner meeting with top officials of the Ministry of Health and Welfare, I spoke out on the issue. "Why is there no separation of powers in Japan?" I queried bluntly.

"Oh, but there is," I was assured. "It's right there in the constitution."

"But surely the reality is different. If the three powers are truly independent, why do we draft legislation?"

"The politicians write laws too, you know."

"But percentage-wise, the vast majority of laws are written by bureaucrats. I'm speaking in terms of substance, not form. As I see it, our basic job is to run the country on the basis of law, while the task of lawmaking belongs, or should belong, to the Diet members."

"You're right about that. Unfortunately, most Diet members lack the ability to write laws."

"Do they see lawmaking as their main duty?"

"In principle, yes. In fact, however, their main duty is to procure benefits for their local districts, like a new bridge or a bullet train line."

"In the United States, it's true that the ability to do things like attract foreign enterprises to your state is an important political asset. But anybody who's incapable of making a law just isn't qualified to serve in the House."

"Oh, they could make laws if they tried. The Diet does have its own bureau of legislation. It's just that—and this is strictly off the record, mind you—the people working there can't compete with the bureaucracy in legislative ability. The cabinet legislation bureau contains the ablest minds in the bureaucracy. So even when a Diet member does come up with a piece of legislation, it's not as well crafted. Take a look for yourself sometime. The legislation they draft is full of holes. It's got so many loopholes, it's a regular sieve. The Regulation of Money for Political Activities Act is a prime example."

"Weird. Tell me something. I know the cabinet legislation bureau consists of bureaucrats on loan from each government agency, but what about the Diet bureau of legislation? Does that also consist of loaned bureaucrats?"

"Yes."

"If that's the case, why should the lawmaking ability of people in the Diet bureau of legislation be inferior?"

"That's a tough question. For one thing, the Diet legislation bureau is smaller in scale. For another, as you say, they account for only a small percentage of the total in absolute terms, so their people have a lot less work to do than their counterparts in the cabinet legislation bureau, who must always be on their toes. The difference is reflected in the quality of their work. Besides, the most talented people naturally get sent to the cabinet legislation bureau."

"Why is that?"

"This may sound strange, but it'd suit us just fine if the Diet members stayed the way they are."

"As legislators without legislative ability, you mean?"

"In a manner of speaking, yes. Power to run the country on the basis of law is one thing, you see, but power to create the laws is greater by far."

"I agree. And nobody likes to relinquish power. That's a universal truth. So the heart of the matter is that the bureaucracy wants to stay on top, holding on to its power with an iron grip."

"That's a rather drastic way of putting it, but you could look at it that way, yes."

The Absolute Sway of the Bureaucrats

"But the reason separation of powers is stipulated in the Constitution," I continued, "is that concentration of powers leads to abuse; isn't that the underlying idea? With as much power concentrated in the Japanese bureaucracy as there is today, abuse has to be a factor."

"Japan has functioned very well under the present system. Think about it. Can you really imagine today's politicians entrusted with the job of lawmaking? It would be the end of Japan!"

"I'm not all that knowledgeable about the lawmaking system in Japan, but I'll admit you have a point."

"Of course I do. Some of them are not much better than *yakuza*."

"Watching the live telecasts, I've been surprised a number of times to think these are the people who represent their constituents. In the United States or the United Kingdom, if you evaluated them on the basis of intelligence, most would fall, shall we say, short of the mark. Some are outstanding, of course."

"Yes, but politics is a numbers game," he said. "A few outstanding politicians don't make much of a dent. Given the current level of politicians, bureaucrats really have no choice but to shoulder responsibility for Japan."

"I see what you mean. Even if ten percent of the Diet members rate a score of one hundred, the rest probably hover around twenty, so the average score is still abysmal."

"Right. The only reason I don't dismiss the place outright, the way you do, is that even the worst Diet members are still the people's choice. They do deserve that much respect."

"Tell me something else," I said. "Wouldn't it be natural for someone in the bureaucracy to point out the dangers of such a concentration of power?"

"Be realistic. You know as well as I do that once people secure power, they don't give it up easily. The bureaucracy's concentration of power is a problem for the politicians to get off their bottoms and solve."

"But judging from experience, it's impossible for politicians to reform themselves. The people who elect them are equally to blame for the situation. Anyway, if you're right, the absolute sway of the bureaucracy will never change."

"That's Japan for you. You have to get a clear grasp of the situation and then take action in keeping with the current realities. An ability to do that is vital for a bureaucrat. You're just back from the States, where things are different, so you're talking in impracticalities now. Believe me, if you keep up your questioning you'll be thrown out on your ear. Criticizing the bureaucracy is like cutting off your nose to spite your face."

"Thanks for the warning. It's just that I didn't come here out of any desire to make laws. I'm only asking some basic questions."

"Well, it does no harm to talk it over privately like this, but you mustn't ever say such things in public."

"I understand."

Parliamentary Questions

I realize that my sort of idealistic thinking doesn't do much good in the Diet atmosphere I've described. Back to reality.

As soon as the identity of the parliamentarian who will do the interrogating is known, bureaucrats rush off to ferret out the content of the following day's questions.

Why the hurry? It's because for each line of questioning, we have to make up a set of ten to twenty possible questions and answers. If the committee is large and the questions fairly wide-ranging, the resulting guide can easily become the size of a fat book.

Moreover, because of the characteristically Japanese conception of harmony, fine-tuning and behind-the-scenes negotiating become necessary should the content of the replies happen to range over various sections, departments, or even ministries. Such activities account for the bulk of the time it takes to make up the book, at what amounts to a colossal waste of time. Still, whatever it takes, the job has to be finished by the following morning, and so the sooner the questions can be procured, the better.

In addition to all the other maneuvering that goes on, the final product must bear the imprimatur of the Finance Ministry. This is because replies to parliamentary interpellation often have an impact on the budget for the upcoming year. To prevent someone from unwittingly committing himself to a budgetary increase, all answers with a financial angle are sent to the Ministry of Finance for careful scrutiny. This is the last stage in the writing process. By two or three A.M., or even later, final approval is obtained. Then comes the task of binding it all into book form.

Typically, the whole operation lasts until just before dawn. Section chiefs are required to help with the bookbinding, so, as a matter of course, they must spend the night at the office. And since this all falls in the category of voluntary overtime done in a spirit of willing self-sacrifice for the good of the organization, there is no question of remuneration for overtime. After staying up working all night without pay, bureaucrats rub their sleepy eyes and start in on the morning's work as usual.

This may explain much of the infamous inefficiency of administrative services in general. Still, as long as the attention of government administrators is focused not on the nation but on the Diet, there can be little hope that things will ever change.

Political parties differ strikingly in their approach to question-gatherers. Members of the Liberal Democratic Party confide the contents of their questions right down to the fine details. What's more, the questions they eventually ask are identical to the ones they submit beforehand, so that there are no surprises for the bureaucrats. Bureaucrats and LDP politicians play right into each other's hands.

The Democratic Socialist Party of Japan (DSPJ) will reveal the general drift or tenor of their intended queries, but when actual questioning gets underway, the questions tend to be nit-picky, with no apparent relation to what they had promised. The Japan Communist Party, which maintains the farthest distance from the party in power, gives the ministries short shrift, seldom if ever sharing anything about its prospective questions. With the JCP, however, the disdain is mutual.

I am fully aware that the Diet is the highest organ of national power. But all too often, "highest" is taken to mean "sacred." When, for whatever reason, a bureaucrat is occasionally unable to answer a question, members react as if their purity has been sullied. Often, the Diet will actually adjourn—just like the spoiled kid who walks away from the game if he doesn't like the way it's going. It makes no sense. The players in this game are human beings, not supercomputers. Why shouldn't there be questions bureaucrats are unable to answer? Such a common-sense view does not prevail in the Diet, however. And so we bureaucrats prepare answers that are at once solemn and safe, answers that will not cause the speaker to lose face. I often think to myself how hard it is to satisfy a narcissist.

A Game of Old Maid

At one point in a question-gathering mission I had been assigned, a Diet member remarked, "You know, I'm a little out of my depth in this area. Why don't you guys make up a question for me?" No sooner were the words out of his mouth than an official beside me said respectfully, "How about something along these lines, sir?" and proceeded to suggest a highly on-target question.

The nature of the Diet question-and-answer procedure had plagued me from the beginning, but I was even more taken aback by this exchange. The politician responsible for asking questions was asking those responsible for answering them to supply their own questions! The one good thing about it was that it obviated the need for making up a voluminous book of answers to possible questions.

Back at the ministry, I conveyed my surprise to my colleagues, who informed me calmly that the practice was common among members of the ruling party. "A lot of those guys care more about being on camera than they do about the content of their questions," someone added.

I didn't follow. "Why should they care about being on TV?"

"Think about it. It's the ideal way for them to appeal to their constituents, and it doesn't them cost a dime. Back home, the locals brag about seeing 'their boy' on TV. So when the parliamentary proceedings are being televised, everybody gets more animated than usual." Live coverage of the Diet sessions is an effective form of self-advertising, I discovered.

In any case, once the next day's probable questions have been obtained, the secretariat apportions them out among the various ministry departments—a very lengthy process. Now begins the equivalent of a game of Old Maid, each department wanting to avoid getting stuck with the job: "Here, these questions should go to your people." "No, that's out of our jurisdiction." After all, nobody is eager to stay late just to write a bookful of dry, empty statements.

Once the Old Maid game is over and the work has finally been assigned, the task of writing the answers gets underway. Here is where government bureaucrats use up most of their energy. My experience of participating in this exercise taught me that certain basic rules are involved; a certain know-how is essential. First, statements must be noncommittal and worded in such a way that any clear assignment of responsibility becomes impossible. Second, statements should support the status quo. Third, they should be as innocuous and inoffensive as possible. Fourth, answers to sharp, pointed questions should be framed in such a way that they evade the issue without really seeming to.

To satisfy these requirements for all questions we come up against—many of them hair-splitting—is a herculean task. The finished product is generally as tasteless and unpalatable as gum that has been chewed for an hour.

DietSpeak

Once, as I was struggling to frame a reply to a certain question, one of my superiors remarked sympathetically, "You've got to use the right wording. Here, read this." He handed me a guide-book—not an official ministry publication, of course, but an unofficial pony that circulates among bureaucrats. I found that it shed considerable light on the essence of the Diet interpellation system. At the risk of earning the approbation of my colleagues for divulging its contents—like a magician giving away tricks of the trade—let me illustrate just some of it.

The word *maemuki ni*, which means "positively" or "constructively," is calculated to give listeners faint hope that something may possibly transpire in the distant future, although there are no immediate prospects. *Eii*, the word for "assiduous" or "energetic," is used when prospects are poor, but you want to impress listeners with your efforts. The word *jubun* (fully, thoroughly) is useful when you want to stall for time, and *tsu-tomeru*, to endeavor, means that you take no responsibility. The expression *hairyo suru*, literally to give something your "careful consideration," actually means letting it stay indefinitely on your desk without ever taking any action. Similarly, *kento suru* (investigate, look into) means to kick something around but do nothing. *Mimamoru* (follow closely) means you will assign it to others and do nothing yourself. The expression *okiki suru*, or "respectfully listen," likewise means you will only listen, and do nothing. Finally, *shincho ni*, or "cautiously," is used when things are virtually hopeless but you can't come right out and say so; it means that nothing will be done.

In the morning, the answers, which have been painstakingly put together all night long in this fashion, are explained to Cabinet members, director generals, and whoever else will actually be responding to questioning. Both questions and answers in Diet sessions are thus almost entirely scripted.

Some respondents, however, are extremely quick-thinking and lucid. During the revision of the Mental Health Law, we were handed this question beforehand: "What do the mentally handicapped mean to you?" Not only was the question vague, but it was intended for the prime minister. We racked our brains, and came up with a lengthy, voluminous reply. The next day, however, the prime minister summed it up in two succinct words: "Human rights." Our whole division was filled with admiration.

Special care goes into the writing of the prime minister's answers. We cover every angle we can think of, knowing that a slip-up could well cost one of us a promotion. To my surprise, I also found that only the prime minister's answers are written in large, bold type. I once asked someone the reason.

"That's because he's in a category all his own. His status is expressed through the size of the characters. The real reason, though, is that by the time a man gets to be prime minister, his eyesight is often weak. Even with characters that big, sometimes a prime minister will still manage to skip lines while reading."

I remember being intrigued by the discovery that the prime minister's responses to Diet questioning encapsulate the issue on which the Ministry of Health and Welfare puts greatest emphasis: measures to deal with the rapid aging of Japanese society.

Diet interrogations involve replies that are scripted by bureaucrats in line with official dogma and read aloud by parliamentarians who perform like veteran actors. Bureaucrats and Diet members alike have their allotted roles to play, and *honne*—what people really think—never takes center stage. It makes its entrance only backstage in high-priced Japanese restaurants, spoken in hushed tones. This is how the Diet really works.

The Democracy of Unanimity

The Diet is supposed to be a bastion of free debate, a place where elected representatives of the people carry on thorough-going debates as part of their legislative work. In fact, however, the substantive, logical give-and-take of Western-style debate is seldom seen because most lawmaking is left in the hands of the bureaucrats.

Moreover, it is assumed in Japan that Diet resolutions ought to pass unanimously—in spite of the inherent impossibility of hundreds of opinions coinciding exactly with hundreds of others. Unlike the West, where dissent is regarded as the sign of a healthy, functioning democracy, Japan considers consensus to be the foundation of democracy. Any resolution that passed unanimously, without one dissenting vote, would be seen as swayed by prejudice or emotion anywhere in the West.

It seems self-evident that democracy functions best when free and open debate can be carried on without the slightest concern for what anyone may think. The scope of this problem in Japan goes far beyond the national Diet. Almost nowhere in Japanese society do you find people arguing down their opponents in an open forum using the free exchange of logical debate.

"Are You Trying to Pick a Fight With Me?"

Not long after my return to Japan, I had occasion to meet with colleagues to discuss the future of mental health care across the country. During the course of the discussion, I made the following statement to one colleague: "I'm afraid I cannot agree with you. For this, this, and this reason your analysis is faulty, and therefore I have doubts about the reliability of your conclusions." I had no doubt that he would reply by pointing out difficulties in my own logical construct, and that we would go at it from there.

To my amazement, he retorted, "Are you trying to pick a fight with me?" Since I certainly was not doing any such thing, I quickly persuaded him of my peaceful intentions and managed to patch things up—but we remained on cool terms from then on. After several more such blunders, I began to see why it is that Japanese make such a careful distinction between *tatemae*, or the official stance, and *honne*, what they really think or feel: they want at all cost to avoid a conflict involving aggressive emotions such as anger and envy.

No such distinction is sanctioned in the West, where people are accustomed from a very early age to using logic in their dealings with one another and have accordingly mastered techniques of controlling their anger and envy. Generally, they do not flinch if someone says no to them, and they are capable of saying no to others without fear. The ability to do so is indeed a passport into adult society.

In Japan, on the other hand, people go out of their way to avoid saying no. Because Japanese are not used to handling their feelings of aggression, they are helpless once those emotions are released. An unconscious awareness of this peculiarity explains the development in Japanese culture of *tatemae* and *honne*, which allow people to seek leniency (*amae*) from one another. From the Western point of view, however, the culture of mutual leniency, based on a division between official truth and actual truth, is infantile.

During one all-night Diet session on the PKO (United Nations Peacekeeping Operations) resolution, a journalist friend of mine grumbled with a look of exhaustion, "Forced votes, 'cow-walks,'* resignations . . . why on earth are Japanese legislators so childish? This is supposed to be a bastion of free speech, but nobody tries to have a forceful exchange of opinion or to seek common ground for discussion. All anybody wants to do is fight to push through his high-sounding agenda and make himself look good."

Democracy in a place where representatives push through their agendas with other representatives who believe in consensus across party lines is not worth much. Anyone who thinks the Japanese Diet is a democratic institution—including its members—needs to do a little reading and thinking and learn what democracy is all about.

I often forget that I'm a bureaucrat myself, and that I'd be better off not violating the quaint old custom that bureaucrats never criticize members of the Diet or, God forbid, political parties. I will just mention that even after the five-day work-week was introduced for civil servants in May 1992, Diet staff workers are still forced to put in night after night of sleepless,

---

* "Cow-walk" refers to a delaying tactic taken by Japanese opposition parties who want to stall the passage of legislation. By taking several hours to walk up to the Diet podium to deliver their vote, they aim to block legislation through lengthy delays.

self-sacrificing service, and countless government officials are then forced to match that pace. All, naturally, without a single voice of complaint.

The Pecking Order

A brief description of the structure of the ministries and the loan system of personnel exchange is in order here. Each ministry is a vertical hierarchy headed by a minister, followed in order by a vice-minister, director general, administrative chief, departmental chief, director, deputy director, section chief, clerks, and part-time female workers.

Vice-ministerial posts are of two varieties: administrative, the highest decision-making authority in the ministry, and parliamentary, a post that is given only to politicians who have been reelected more than once. Supposedly the two posts have equal authority, but in fact the latter is handed to up-and-coming politicians to make them look more important. Appointees tend to be mere ornamental figureheads, without much say. This explains why they are known derisively as the "appendix" of the ministry.

Next is the director general. Each bureau has its own head; in the Ministry of Health and Welfare, there are nine. There are seven administrative chiefs and two departmental chiefs. These officials function as the rudder to determine the overall direction in which the ministries will move, as well as being responsible for adjustment between politicians and industry and laying the groundwork for a consensus.

Posts of administrative chief on up, known as designated posts, have the greatest prestige. Such high-ranking officials have the privilege of riding in black government limousines and boast offices that are fairly large, if dreary. They also receive substantially higher salaries and pensions than their colleagues in nondesignated posts and are able to retire to more desirable posts in private industry; their total retirement package goes way up.

For all those reasons, nothing arouses such intense interest among bureaucrats as the competition for high-ranking posts. Self-importance—that they feel, as members of the top brass of Japan, Inc. who bear the country's burdens,—also becomes an important life goal for aspiring bureaucrats. In order to attain one of these coveted posts, however, it is necessary to pass the highest-level civil service examination (currently Type I). Those who do are known as career officials.

I am what is known as a technical official. Technical officials include all sorts of professionals, including doctors, dentists, pharmacists, veterinarians, nurses, and sanitary engineers. As a doctor, I belong to the group known as medical technical officials. Doctors, because they have passed the National Examination for Medical Practitioners, are treated on par with career officials. They may head any of four bureaus: the Health Policy Bureau, the Health Service Bureau, the Air Quality Bureau, and the Environmental Health Bureau. Of these, the Air Quality Bureau is part of the Environment Agency, but it is ranked above the Environmental Health Bureau. There is, however, one difference between medical technical officials and career officials: medical technical officials cannot become vice-minister.

All other bureaucrats are known as noncareer officials. They are by far the greatest in number. With luck, about the time they are ready for retirement they may make section chief in their home ministry, but for the most part, they are given administrative posts in extraministerial bureaus. That the ministries function properly is due in large part to their efforts.

The Almighty Director

The Ministry of Health and Welfare contains about one hundred administrative posts. Administrative posts differ from other posts in two respects: those in them are entitled to a special monthly recompense, and they lose their right to be paid for overtime. In point of fact, it means simply that all overtime becomes unpaid "voluntary overtime." In the world of official-dom, however, where rank means everything, no one complains. Instead, they gloat at being told, "Hey, aren't you doing well for yourself! One of these days we'll see you in a designated post!"

Why do private citizens bow and scrape to ministry direc-tors? Because most divisions have jurisdiction over laws giving them executive authority over industrial and business organiza-tions. The exercise of this authority can be a matter of life and death for the organizations concerned. Power is concentrated in the hands of the director, who, accordingly, is held in awe.

The pecking order among directors is determined by length of service in the ministry. The heads of the three divisions in the Minister's Secretariat—general affairs, accounts, and per-sonnel—each get the use of a limousine and their own private office. They may be thought of as the extreme right flank of the top officials. Below them are the heads of the planning and general affairs divisions of each bureau.

Among the medical technical officials, the ranking goes like this: the Welfare Science Division of the Minister's Secretariat, followed by the Planning Division of the Health Policy Bureau and the Service Division of the Health Insurance Bureau. Below these, evenly matched, are the Administrative Guidance Division of the National Hospitals and the Disease Control Division of the Health Service Bureau. Then there are the people assigned to reception of section chiefs, with titles like coordinator, planner, investigator, and promoter.

Why should such neither-here-nor-there posts be necessary? Because in the government ministries, seniority is everything. When someone is promoted to an administrative post, those admitted to the ministry at the same time require the same sort of treatment. Despite the subtle difference in ranking, outbreaks of envy can be prevented by giving everyone titles that are apparently on the same level. The ministry can be thought of, however, as an aggregate of small villagelike organizations—the career officials, medical practitioners, pharmacists, veterinarians, nurses, noncareer officials, and so on—each of which has its own path to success. They can be thought of as so many factions. The Office of Disease Control, for example, is always headed by a medical practitioner and never by anyone from a different group. Naturally enough, as doctors, we are assigned to positions where our specialized medical knowledge can come into play. The other factions, however, are constantly on the lookout for ways to enlarge their influence, and hence compete among themselves for available posts.

The reason that top medical officials took such umbrage at my disruption of faction harmony was simple: they knew that those in the career faction could well take advantage of such disarray to grab extra posts for themselves. That underlying fear produced a loud chorus of criticism.

Section Dynamics

Beneath the all-powerful director are the deputy directors, whose number depends on the size of the division. The senior deputy directors are at the top of the hierarchy. Often, however, there will be three senior deputy directors; one is a career-track job, while the other two are noncareer medical and administrative officials. They compete among themselves for promotion, but their competition tends to degenerate into attempts to trip one another up. (Resentment toward medical officials is particularly intense. Amazing at it may seem, medical officials must be prepared to expend enormous amounts of energy handling the envy that will come their way if they expect to see their ideas reflected in national policy.)

Beneath the deputy director is the section chief. It is the section chief who, generally, deals with the public. Offend him and you'll never get the permit you're after, which is why people in the private sector kowtow to him. The idea of bureaucrats as public servants does not necessarily accord with reality, as an encounter with a section chief can quickly establish.

Next in line are a group of young men in their mid-twenties whose tastes and ideals tend to differ from those of their more staid and traditional elders. Still, they are the ones who do the bulk of the work. They, too, end up falling in with traditional ways despite themselves, reluctantly staying at their desks until all hours to avoid the wrath of their boss. The youth of these hapless young men, who have no time for any social life, is effectively stolen by the bureaucracy.

Below them in the hierarchy are the women who serve tea, make copies, and do odd jobs; generally, each division has one. Most are young and unmarried, and their most pressing goal seems to be finding a husband. As a result, they perform thankless tasks that make no use of their abilities, and they receive far lower wages than their male counterparts, all without a word of complaint. They have the "privilege" of going home at quitting time, so that after five o'clock the offices turn into a male-only, quasi-homosexual society.

In the bureaucracy, each person has a distinct role to play and must do so to the best of his ability. The "privilege" of being allowed to leave the office premises gives a clear indication of the role women play in Japanese society. It is in fact a subtle form of discrimination, but I will have more to say on this subject later.

Personnel Loans

The government ministries have a unique personnel system which carries out temporary exchanges of personnel at the national and prefectural levels. The Ministry of Health and Welfare, for example, sends employees on loan to the Cabinet, the Prime Minister's Office, the Finance Ministry, the Ministry of Foreign Affairs, the Ministry of Home Affairs, the Ministry of Justice, the Ministry of Education, the Defense Agency, the National Police Agency, the Economic Planning Agency, the Fire Defense Agency, the prefectures, corporations with special status, embassies and legations abroad, the World Health Organization (WHO), the World Bank, and other institutions. In fact, we can safely say that the Health and Welfare Ministry has representatives at all levels of the central government.

How did this system come into place? It began as a way for upper-echelon bureaucrats to request expert assistance in needed areas on a temporary basis, usually about two years. After the two years expire, a new person is sent over to do the same job. Any agency or institution that receives such personnel on loan, moreover, reciprocates in kind. Whether there is an exchange of personnel of the same level depends on the balance of power between the two institutions.

Such exchanges also contribute to a general broadening of perspective. The clearest example of this may be seen in the top personnel appointments of a new agency, as in the founding a few years back of the Defense Agency, when top posts were filled by people from the Ministry of Finance, the National Policy Agency, and the Ministry of Health and Welfare. But the biggest advantage in such exchanges of personnel lies in the chance for different agencies to learn about one another and deepen mutual understanding, creating solid horizontal links in the vertical hierarchy of the bureaucracy.

The personnel exchange system can be likened to joint sharing of stock: just as two corporations can supplement and strengthen each other by mutual ownership, so the sharing of personnel serves to deepen and strengthen ties among participating institutions and creates a sense of unity.

A Communications Network Based on En

The basic stance of a bureaucrat is "never reveal more than absolutely necessary." Due to the demerit system of rating, your career will suffer should problems arise from something you once said. In addition, there is a clear line in the bureaucratic world separating "inside" from "outside" Inevitably, those who are perceived as "outsiders" are treated with greater coolness.

An analysis of the phenomenon of personnel loans in psychological terms reveals a close connection to the psychology of *en* (bond or affinity.) Sending employees to outside organizations is a way of building *en* with them. The presence or absence of *en* is always a determining factor in Japanese relationships. The common proclivity for differentiating between inside and outside is even more pronounced between collective organizations, leading to corresponding difficulties in communication. Yet for the collective entity of Japan itself to function smoothly, adequate communication is a must. The best way to facilitate communication is to create ties that serve as a bridge between inside and out. The system of personnel loans is admirably suited to this purpose.

The bureaucracy has other ways of doing the same thing. Month-long personnel seminars are held, involving people from every ministry and agency; one for directors, another for deputy directors, and so on. Time spent together in this way also creates strong, resilient bonds across institutions.

These methods of creating *en* also mean that a highly effective communication network is in place all across the country. The merit of this system becomes evident when a new policy is to be implemented. Information is instantly accessible between the relevant ministries and agencies across Japan. The efficiency of the system is miles ahead of any information-gathering techniques in the private sector. Moreover, because the bureaucracy takes full advantage of other types of cliques as well—such as those based on academic background or birth-place—the amount of information that may be accessed is mind-boggling. In that sense, the bureaucracy is fully comparable to the CIA or KGB.

The vast amount of available information translates into greater speed and ease in implementing new policy decisions. Any time there is a shift in policy, extensive *nemawashi*, or "behind-the-scenes negotiations," must take place. The personnel loan system ensures smooth *nemawashi* across various ministries, so that new policies can be put into effect without fomenting large-scale resistance. In fact, it wouldn't be an exaggeration to say that personnel loans are the greatest strength of the bureaucracy.

The system is not without its problems, however. Even when a post has lost its significance due to societal or other changes, bureaucratic conservatism and reverence for precedent make the post virtually impossible to abolish. "Protect your vested rights at all costs" is the golden rule of bureaucrats. Losing a vested right is the biggest black mark a bureaucrat could possibly acquire. Bureaucrats are forced to hang on stubbornly to their turf in order to protect their own necks. The result is that a given post remains in effect regardless of its importance or status. Needless to say, the cost of all this is borne by the taxpayer.

In 1957, history professor C. Northcote Parkinson took advantage of his experience as a British Army staff officer during World War II to publish his "Parkinson's Law": "The number of bureaucrats will go on increasing regardless of the amount of work to be done." The Japanese bureaucracy fits Professor Parkinson's description to a tee.

Welcome to Groupism

First, the Beer

In government offices in Japan, fall is the season of the annual office trip. The second week after I joined the Ministry of Health and Welfare as deputy director, I was accosted by the trip manager.

"We'll be going to Whatchamacallit Hot Spring in November this year. What do you want to do about transportation? Just about everybody is taking the train."

In my ignorance I asked, "Will that be on a weekday?"

"No, we go on a weekend," came the answer. He then further explained, "We do this once a year, to encourage feelings of fellowship among the section members. We solicit opinions from everyone in the early spring and then decide where to go."

"So participation is optional?" I made a point of asking.

"Yes, in principle, but it's customary for everyone to go, unless they're sick or something."

"Why foster feelings of fellowship on a weekend?" I asked.

"Weekdays we're so busy there's no time for travel, so that leaves the weekend. People are really looking forward to it."

What the chief clerk wanted to know was not whether or not I would be going, but only what sort of transportation I would prefer. He made it sound as if my going was a matter of course. At this point I was still a novice. I told him I would go on the train with everyone else, feeling in part that, after eleven years away, it would be nice to soak in a hot spring and soak up the atmosphere of traditional Japan. Later on, during the trip, I was to find out just how ridiculously wide of the mark my expectations were.

First, the train trip down. We had virtually a whole car reserved for ourselves. After hastily finishing up the morning's work, we all piled aboard a train scheduled to leave at two. Within minutes, cans of beer were being passed around.

"I'll hold off till we get there," I said, but they would have none of that: "Now, don't be shy, everyone's drinking. If you don't want beer, we've got *shochu* and *saké* as well."

An hour later, nearly everyone was inebriated. Magazines purchased in the station had been spread out, and the nude photographs in them were under heated appraisal. For me alone to contribute nothing to the discussion would have seemed churlish, so I offered my comments, along these lines:

"These photos emphasize sex in a licentious sort of way; if the photographer had let his individuality interact more with the model, they'd be more alive, wouldn't they?"

As if to let me know how out of place my remarks were, my co-workers heaped scorn on me: "Lighten up, Miyamoto! Get off your high horse and drink up. You can impress us with your education and intelligence some other time. This is Japan. You're not Japanese enough yet by a long shot."

Worse, I was then subjected to a barrage of questions that amounted to an infringement of privacy: "How is sex different among Americans and Japanese?" they wanted to know, among other things. Gradually the conversation centered on blunt talk about sex; the drunker everyone got, the cruder the level of discussion.

Don't get me wrong. I'm a normal male, with a normal interest in talking about sex. Even so, I found myself hard pressed to keep up with such out-and-out coarseness. Accustomed as I was to the conversation of Westerners, which, however erotic in content, is laced with amusing touches of wit, I found something sad in the display being put on by my peers.

The Yukata and the Red Sweater

Eventually we arrived at the hot spring. At last, I thought, a chance to savor the tasteful atmosphere of traditional Japan— but again, I was to find my expectations way off base. Our inn featured a souvenir stand in the entryway. Bright fluorescent lights lit up every corner, just like the office. Computer blips from the video-game room filled my ears. To me, the words "Japanese inn" had suggested the world of understated beauty memorialized in novelist Jun'ichiro Tanizaki's essay *In Praise of Shadows*—a world of soothing lantern-light; of gardens with flowing streams where, now and again, bamboo devices gave off an appealing sound; of the strains of soft *koto* music; and of the subtle fragrance of incense. All of these naive expectations marked me indubitably as a "foreigner."

Without the least apparent regard for my letdown, my colleagues rushed off excitedly for the bath, unwilling to linger for even a few minutes in their rooms. As I found out afterwards, one of the main attractions of this hot spring was mixed bathing. No one in our group ever indicated, however, that they'd found any beauties in the bath worth getting excited about. Some members were not easily reconciled, however, and hovered nearly two hours in the hot waters, clustered in the shadows of big rocks, hoping against hope. Apparently, the more serious they are normally, the more daffy they get on such occasions.

A sober look around the bathing area, undeluded by the false promise of "mixed bathing," revealed it to be a hot spring in name only, as the water in the baths was merely pumped up and reheated. The decor, moreover, consisted of dreary tiles and fake-looking rock mountains. The average Tokyo public bath has far more atmosphere.

Soon we received word to gather in the banquet room. As I started out the door of my room in a sweater and jeans, someone stopped me and told me that I was supposed to wear a *yukata*—the thin kimono provided for each guest. But this was toward the end of November, and there was a chill in the air. I dislike the cold, and so to keep myself warm after the bath, I had no choice but to wear a heavy sweater underneath my *yukata* and pull on a pair of thick knee socks. Thus attired, I set off for the banquet hall.

As the only one with a red sweater showing at the neck of his *yukata* and patterned socks on his feet, I was the focus of curious stares. For my part, as a newcomer to such occasions, the sight of so many people all wearing identical *yukata* struck me as indescribably odd. But as I later learned, dressing alike for dinner is customary at a hot-springs inn. I couldn't help marveling that the influence of groupism, which runs so deep in so many Japanese, should reveal itself so clearly on such occasions.

At mealtimes, everyone is served exactly the same thing. It's only human to have likes and dislikes, yet individual preferences are totally disregarded. On our trays, what should have been hot was cold, what should have been cold was lukewarm, and all of it was terribly salty. The meal was designed chiefly to look impressive, with a preponderance of shrimp, crab, tempura, and other high-cholesterol foods. And yet the Ministry of Health and Welfare is the nation's highest agency promoting health care. That its employees should unprotestingly eat a meal demonstrating such little concern for health considerations came as a shock to me.

Seated facing this meal, I was reminded of hospital food, with its three unfailing attributes: fast, cold, and unpalatable. No wonder hospital food never shows any improvement, I thought, if Health and Welfare Ministry employees will not voice a single complaint over food served to them on an office trip aimed at their own well-being! Yet there we were, in our matching *yukata*, lined up facing our unpalatable dinners. We looked like broilers in a poultry farm.

If I may jump ahead in my story, when the third of these section safaris came around, I couldn't bear the thought of another lousy meal and privately telephoned ahead to the inn where we would be staying (with silent apologies to the fellow in charge of arrangements) to ask if they would please see that hot foods were served hot. The response was as follows:

"We have never received such a request in all the years we have been in business. Our prices are so low anyway that it's difficult to say if we could meet your request."

Not to be deterred, I shot back, "What I am asking is extremely simple. Good food has to be prepared with loving care. That's all I am saying. Food that is prepared from the heart naturally tastes better. For example, instead of using frozen shrimp to make the dinner look impressive, try fresh sardines or sweetfish. Don't cook for show, cook from the heart." Then I hung up.

When the day of the banquet rolled around, it seemed that my conversation with the proprietress had borne some fruit, for all the food was served at the proper temperature. The special of the day, however, was fresh-fried tempura, with each shrimp in a coating so heavy it appeared to be wearing a padded jacket. As we were in fact all wearing padded jackets at the time, this struck me as quite funny. In any case, the experience taught me again the importance of speaking up with an opinion.

Later, when I told the fellow in charge what I had done, he said, "So that explains it. I knew the service was better than usual. It's amazing, though, that an inn that always offers the same thing to every guest would even listen to you. What on earth did you tell them?" I will never forget the mixture of admiration and perplexity on his face.

"Drink, Drink!"

After the banquet began, I found myself in for another surprise. People were going around eagerly pouring drinks for one another, scarcely glancing at their food. Clearly, the main purpose of the banquet was not to enjoy one's food but to drink. This explained why the quality of the food was a nonissue.

I patiently explained that I was not a drinker, but such quibbles were swept aside as I was urged, "Drink up, drink up!" Looking around, I saw people thanking the pourer politely every time their glass was filled. I for one was not going to thank anyone for forcing a drink on me that I didn't want and sighed to think this was a Japanese custom. Evidently noticing my troubled expression, someone gave me some advice as he poured me a drink.

"It's not like this in the provinces. There, they have a hole in the *saké*-cup that you have to keep your finger over, or else the *saké* runs out the bottom. It's served good and hot, too, so you'll scald your finger unless you gulp it down fast. Anyway, it's a good idea to train yourself be able to drink."

What a difference in the method of pouring drinks, I

couldn't help thinking. In the West, a sommelier pours wine; to abstain, all you need do is lay your fingers lightly across your wineglass. As a result, it is possible to remain in control of your own drinking. Never are unwanted drinks forced on anyone. In a restaurant without a sommelier, diners may pour drinks for one another, but the same rule applies. The idea of people setting out deliberately to get one another drunk, as they do in Japan, is inconceivable. People assume responsibility for their own level of inebriation and display constant respect for one another. Accustomed to that approach, I was truly amazed by the kind of boozing that went on during this office trip.

The main purpose of the banquet, I soon learned, was to get drunk together. Moreover, I observed that even people whom everyone knew to have a low tolerance of alcohol were forced to drink whether they liked it or not.

"Government officials have to be able to hold their liquor. This is for your own good," such hapless individuals are assured. In fact, however, the sight of one's victim suffering the ill effects of alcohol is a source of endless amusement. Nobody interferes; everyone enjoys the spectacle. In the Japanese world of seniority systems and lifelong employment, when a superior offers to pour you a drink, it's hard to say no.

An Extension of Work

A colleague who heard that I was complaining about company banquets once gave me some advice: "You've got to learn to drink a little bit."

"I can. But I want to drink at my own pace and to choose my own drinks. If I can't, I'd rather not drink at all."

"Don't talk like a spoiled child. The banquet hall is an extension of the workplace. Refusing a cup of *saké* amounts to a rejection of whoever offered it to you. You can't go around hurting people's feelings."

"Why can't the other person take my feelings into consideration?"

"Listen. One of these days, you'll be in charge of the health and sanitation of an entire prefecture. You'll have what amounts to a ministerial position in the prefectural government, so everyone will be watching you. I've been through it myself many times. There are banquets almost every day. But you've got to take into consideration the feelings of those who are entertaining you. It's important to eat whatever they put in front of you, and accept every time they offer you a cup of *saké*. Then you can begin to level with each other, to show each other your true selves. By nurturing relationships like that, you are able to find out what's really on people's minds and deal with it. Only then have you got a prayer of putting into effect any plans you may have. You aren't in the post that long, so if you strain your liver a bit in the process, or gain a few pounds, *c'est la vie*."

I was unconvinced. "The idea of neglecting my health for the sake of my work, or for the sake of someone's feelings, is beyond me. Government policies are important, but my own health comes first."

"You say that because you're just back from America," my friend chided. "You've got to get used to our way of doing things. Unless you change the way you think, you can't survive in Japanese society, and you'll just be a burden to your co-workers."

Scandalous Behavior and Wild Parties

As time went on, the banquet became increasingly rowdy. Some people were chugging *saké* down as if it were a test of manhood. Others were shouting out loud, or drinking stripped to the waist, or dancing in the nude, or drinking themselves into oblivion. I could only sit and wonder about the nature of human dignity.

In a Western-style formal banquet, alcohol increases the humor, esprit, and wit of the conversation. While I do realize that not every issue can be reduced to a simple comparison between Japan and the West, from what I've seen of ministry-sponsored banquets, I would have to say that in this case, the West gets my nod—even though, as one who takes pride in the overall sophistication of Japanese culture, it pains me to admit it.

A bunch of drunken, pot-bellied, middle-aged men whooping it up, with *yukata* in disarray, makes an unimaginably ignominious sight. The only reason they can get away with such escapades is, I think, that women rarely participate.

Close observation reveals that such male-only banquets have two characteristics. For one thing, participants' speech and actions become extremely juvenile. For another, men begin to hang on one another in a way that appears to carry homosexual nuances. Then and only then do they let their *honne*—their gut opinions—out. Everyone's pet dissatisfactions, including criticism of the boss, come flying out in no uncertain terms. Meanwhile the director pretends to be intoxicated, while listening tolerantly with a wry smile.

My habit of speaking my mind when I'm sober has invited criticism and even a measure of ostracism. But in the atmosphere of such a banquet, nothing you say is held against you. Normally, outward harmony is maintained; yet in fact, there is considerable underlying stress. People do have their complaints and dissatisfactions. The annual banquet serves as a safety valve to release the stress that builds up in the shadow of the supposed harmony. Peace is preserved by letting off steam periodically in this way.

Gradually I realized that the more quiet and sober someone was ordinarily, the more likely he was to let his hair down at a banquet. Then, drawing on my knowledge of psychoanalysis to dissect my colleagues' mental state, I began to understand that the more someone gives an impression of being quiet, serious, and well adjusted, the more likely that person is to have an inner accumulation of stress. In a world like the Japanese bureaucracy, hemmed in on all sides by *tatemae* (official reality having little to do with people's experience of reality), the stress is all the greater.

I can see that shenanigans at the annual banquet would be an effective way to release some of that stress. As long as I am not forced to join in, I have no complaint. It's their life. It's just that I myself have no desire whatever to participate.

Odd Man Out

The biggest problem with office drinking parties is that those of us who wish no part in it are forced to join in against our will. "Oh, but we're all one big happy family here," we are told, or "One for all and all for one!" Yet at the same time, newcomers like myself who remain odd men out are bombarded with all sorts of sharply worded barbs. If we should get peeved as a result, or our feelings be hurt, too bad. Such arrogance belies the popular notion of civil servants as "models for the nation."

Let me give an example or two. Even now, should I betray ignorance of, say, an old popular song, people jibe me by calling me Urashima Taro, the Japanese Rip van Winkle who rode off on a sea turtle's back and returned to find his friends and family dead, himself an old man. "Go on back to the Dragon King's palace," they jeer. Should I reveal ignorance of a particular product of some region of Japan, they'll groan, "Miyamoto, you foreigner. How could you not know a thing like that? Must be because of all that Western food you eat. You're not like us, after all." Time after time, comments are made that effectively keep me out of the "village." The effect of such often-made comments was to reinforce my sense of being an outsider. Even without such reminders, I faced a gap of a dozen years that I had to fill in somehow; to be treated with contempt because of it made the struggle that much more exhausting.

It was not until long after I entered the ministry that I realized callous-sounding remarks like these—which were heaped on me in good measure at that initial banquet—were actually intended to hasten my integration into the group.

Male Chauvinism

At any rate, having thus become an instrument for the release of everyone's stress, I evidently was not looking too pleased. When I stepped out into the corridor to go to the toilet, one of the female secretaries (read: tea servers) comforted me with these words: "It's hard on you, isn't it, Dr. Miyamoto—having them say those awful things."

"Wait a minute," I said. "Why aren't you in there with everybody?"

"It's so boring," she explained. "I can't wait to go home."

For all intents and purposes, I realized, the banquet hall was off-limits to women. These girl Fridays did put in an appearance, but one after another they quickly got up and left. The one who had spoken to me was just on her way out to take a walk, she said. The only women who stayed through the entire banquet were the waitresses who brought in the food, and geisha, older women whose services the trip manager had somehow contrived to hire despite our slender budget. The literal meaning of "geisha" is "artist," but these women's function was only to pour drinks, add their intermittent comments to racy talk, and generally liven up the atmosphere for the men.

A friend of mine reports that when his company goes on a trip together, the female employees are required to wear *yukata*, too, so that men can enjoy glimpses of bare feet and legs. One woman whose hobby was jazz dancing was ordered by her boss to perform a dance for the group, dressed in a leotard—and did, reluctantly.

Somebody really needs to take people like these aside and explain the concept of sexual harassment, which has yet to make headway in the ministries. Girlie calendars are everywhere, on desktops and walls, sending an unmistakable message about how women are viewed. Basically, the ministries are male-chauvinist institutions.

Bureaucrats tend to have extremely conservative ideas about women. The overwhelming majority believe that women should concern themselves with housekeeping and childcare. The only exceptions in their minds are those women who serve to please men sexually—bar hostesses, geisha, and the like. No woman employee, no matter how gifted, is considered the equal of the least prepossessing man on the staff. The old belief in *danson johi*—"men are superior, women inferior"—is alive and well in the Japanese bureaucracy.

A top official once took it upon himself to scold me for speaking out too plainly. "We live in a world where men deal in *tatemae*, women in *honne*," he cautioned. "If everyone went around saying exactly what they thought all the time, there'd be nothing but trouble. That's why women can't play a major role. You, Miyamoto, have a habit of saying exactly what's on your mind far more than you should. Don't act like a woman."

His words indicated a clear intent to exclude women from the workplace. Also, it seemed to me he was suggesting that it was up to us bureaucrats to protect the notion that women should be submissive to men.

The Porno Room

After about three hours, the banquet was over. Greatly relieved, I headed back to my room, planning to read a book until bedtime—but I was wrong again. It was enough of a shock to find that six of us were crammed into one room, but I then learned that various group activities were planned for the rest of the evening, and my participation was not optional. There was to be no privacy at all.

Our room was transformed on the spot into the "porno room," where a bunch of us were to sit and watch pornographic videos—the sort of activity that giggly high school kids might get a kick out of, I supposed, but hardly my idea of appropriate activity for grown men. Still, everybody seemed in love with the idea.

"Miyamoto probably isn't up on Japanese porno," somebody suggested, and so they considerately began to fill me in on the background of the Japanese actresses: what other films they'd been in, the men in their lives, and what have you, in impressive detail. I half-listened, until someone asked me to tell about American porno. All right, I thought, I might as well share as much as I knew: the difference between soft porno and hard, questions of porno movies and artistic integrity. Finally, when I started to discuss the porno masterpiece, *The Story of O,* touching on the elegance and masochism of the woman, I realized everybody's eyes were glazing over, their mood spoiled. As we sat there, I remembered something a woman had once told me while I was living in the States: "The very existence of pornographic movies is a sign of contempt for women." At the time I'd privately questioned her logic, but after coming back to Japan I was beginning to see that she had a point.

Meanwhile, the rest of my peers were off enjoying the evening elsewhere, having split up into a striptease group, a karaoke group, and a mah-jongg group. The latter two I could see, but the idea of pornography and striptease shows on a company-sponsored trip was beyond my comprehension. From early afternoon until the middle of the night, practically all anyone had wanted to talk about all day was female anatomy and sex, culminating in these raunchy displays. These bureaucrats, normally so staid and businesslike—right down to the most proper, buttoned-down of them all—were acting obsessed.

Group Training

The Japanese propensity to do things in groups, I couldn't help thinking, was what made it possible for party-goers to flaunt the worst sort of behavior and think nothing of it. The same sensibility allows Japanese men to go off on infamous "sex tours" of Asian countries. Westerners, to be sure, are no saints, but they do have their fun individually, while Japanese act in groups and lose all sense of shame. "Red light: if we all cross together, there's nothing to fear," maintains one popular saying, while an old proverb advises, "On a trip, cast away shame." In a group, and away from the usual setting, anything goes—even the most unbridled behavior.

After midnight, everyone came drifting back to their original rooms, having apparently had their fill of their chosen activity. Bedtime at last, I thought with pleasure, but when I looked at the futon laid out for me, I saw only one cover. I often feel cold in the night, so I asked the maid to bring me another and was laconically informed, "One to a customer."

The argument that people are all accustomed to a different sleeping environment—that we all have different sleep habits and needs—would have gone right by her. I was startled and amused to think that the bureaucratic mentality of always going by the book, without regard for individual differences, had permeated even Japan's hot-springs inns.

Still, the idea of catching a cold in the night did not appeal to me, so I tried again. "Well, now, you sound just like a bureaucrat, sticking hard and fast to the rules like that. That's our specialty, not yours. Surely a fine inn like this prides itself on its service. Just as there are tall people and short people in the world, some of us feel chilly with just one cover. I don't want to catch a cold, so please get me another one, won't you?" She must have thought something I said was funny, because she burst out laughing, and went right off to get me an extra cover.

When I entered the room with my prize, everyone was already fast asleep. Exhausted, for once I was able to fall in with the group quite willingly.

The next day was Sunday. From early in the morning, once again, group activities were planned. With all the commotion of the previous night, I was short on sleep and wished they would let me sleep late, but reveille sounded promptly at seven-thirty. "Dr. Miyamoto, get up right away please, it's time for breakfast." The trip manager instructed everyone to finish eating by eight-thirty. After a free-wheeling night, suddenly it was like the army.

Practically everywhere on my travels in the United States, Europe, and Southeast Asia, breakfast was served until eleven. Some places continued to serve it as late as two. This kind of relaxation is a welcome relief from the hectic pace of daily life. To me, the basic purpose of traveling is to come into contact with a foreign culture, enlarge your acquaintance with the world, and relax.

This office excursion, I was coming to realize, was a totally different affair. The office trip in Japan serves as a kind of training ground for carrying out well-ordered group activities, as well as a mechanism for stress management that allows people to release pent-up stress from daily tensions. An extension of work, in other words.

Enough was enough for me. Now, every time the trip manager comes around to ask if I'll be going along, I always answer this way: "The office trip is an extension of work, so I'll go as long as I can have another day off as compensation. If not, I refuse to give up my Saturday and Sunday for the sake of the organization." The trip manager (a different person every time) never fails to blink in astonishment.

Silent Pressure

During my stint on loan at the Defense Agency, I once said the same thing to my superior: "I don't mind going on the office trip, but I look on it as part of work. Since it takes up an entire weekend, I would like a day and a half off to make up for the time lost. Please tell me the procedure for applying for that time off."

My superior wore a look of amazement. "What are you talking about?" he said. "Everyone looks forward to the office trip. It's an annual event that everyone participates in together. It's certainly not an extension of work. There is no precedent for getting time off in compensation. It's out of the question."

"I don't think you can really say everyone looks forward to it, sir," I argued. "I for one don't enjoy office trips at all."

"Then you needn't attend," was the cold reply.

Pouncing on the inconsistency in what he said, I pointed out, "See, you use the word 'attend.' The fact that in some sense you are taking attendance shows that you do, in fact, see it as part of our work."

"What nonsense are you talking?" he said, angry now.

As long as I'd gone and gotten him angry, I took it a step further. "I'm only stating facts. Besides, I've heard that people who don't go on the office trips lose favor with their superiors."

He looked still more ill-humored. "That's not true at all. You're making something out of nothing."

"Am I? I don't think so. When I was in the Ministry of Health and Welfare, I was forced to go on the office trip more or less against my will. So you see, the office trip has to be seen as part of the job, and not as recreation."

The man made no attempt to hide his displeasure at my logic. "Go read the Government Officials Act," he said curtly. "It doesn't say anywhere that going on office trips is part of your job."

"I'm not talking about the law. In principle what you say is true, but in practice, things are different, aren't they? There is silent pressure to go along on the office trip, and I'm saying that that is a problem. Next, I'm saying that if our behavior is controlled by such silent pressure, then it's only natural to consider what we do during that timespan a part of our work."

This expansion on my pet theory received short shrift. "You're just saying that to suit yourself. If you don't want to go, then don't go. That's all there is to it," he said with a sour look.

This was on the verge of turning into a quarrel. I knew I was treading on thin ice, but having come this far, I couldn't let the matter drop. "I'm afraid it's not that simple. I'm here on loan from another ministry, so if I have a difference of opinion with you it doesn't really matter in the long run. Most government officials, however, would undoubtedly seek to avoid a run-in with their boss. Those people would have no choice but to go on the trip, even if they didn't really want to. It's partly for their sakes that I'm pointing out this problem."

"You don't have to go around poking your nose into other people's business." In other words, shut up. Never one to give up easily, however, I pressed on.

"I'm not so sure about that. People's individual rights are being denied. If I say nothing, in the end my own rights will be denied. That's why I have to speak out."

The more logical I became, the more irritated he looked. "Look, this isn't a matter of rights or duties. You're too argumentative. If you keep on this way after you go back to the Ministry of Health and Welfare, you'll never amount to anything."

Now he was getting nasty. There was no turning back. I decided to finish up with a clear statement of where I stood. "I appreciate the warning. But my private time is very important to me. It's not something I can give up lightly for the sake of the organization. Anyway, this problem comes out of a basic difference in our views of life, if you ask me. I'm sorry we can't find a common meeting ground. Apparently there is no point in continuing the discussion. In any case, I have no intention of altering my view that the office trip is an extension of work. And so, if I can't get extra time off in compensation, I have no choice but to decline to participate."

"Suit yourself," he said, and turned away in a huff.

The fellow whose desk was next to mine had apparently overheard my argument with the senior official and sympathized with my side; he told me the history of the institution of the office trip: "It got started after the war, when the ministry set aside a certain amount of money each month to subsidize a trip so that the people working so hard to rebuild Japan might have a chance to rest once a year. Times have changed, but traditions die hard. There are a lot of people who don't really want to go."

That made sense. The trip was a relic of an era when people had no time for themselves. To hang on to it stubbornly now seemed at cross-purposes with the administration's avowed intent of creating a "lifestyle superpower," as they like to call it, in which every person has ample leisure time.

It's Not Right for One Person to Go Alone

At nine, after breakfast on Day Two of the original trip, we were given an explanation of the day's schedule. Which would I prefer to join, I was asked, the golf group, the pleasure boat group, the sightseeing group, or the group planning a visit to a wine factory? There didn't seem to be a "none-of-the-above" option. Once again, there was no freedom of the individual.

Since I myself wanted nothing more than to get out of there as soon as possible, it occurred to me that there might be others who felt the same way. I decided to test the theory, and announced that I would be leaving on the ten o'clock train. As I set about preparing to leave, ignoring the surprised looks of my co-workers, someone else spoke up. "Shall I go with you, then? It's not right for one person to go alone." Other sympathizers appeared. They leaped at my words, using them as a pretext to escape. Alas, hemmed in by the group control system of life-time employment and seniority, the poor devils had been trained never to volunteer an opinion. In the end, about five people left with me. My hypothesis had been correct.

The office trip demonstrates in a nutshell the basic problems with the bureaucratic system and the tendency for people to act in concert: In the name of tradition, an anachronistic system reigns supreme, and individual members of the group keep a close eye on one another; as a result, even if someone has an opinion of his own, he dare not utter it for fear of what people will say. Individual thought is suppressed in the cause of pre-serving the traditions of the organization. Even if many people realize that the practice is anachronistic, they are powerless to change it. All of this is true of much else besides the office trip.

This discovery was the single benefit I gained from going on the office trip.

The Rite
of Budget
Revision

Free Talking

In the ministries, budget revision is the next important event after the Diet sessions. Accordingly, it is always given top priority—even after 6:00 P.M.

"Say, Miyamoto, we'll be having our first free-talking session this evening on the budget, so be sure to save time for it."

The message was clear: this meeting is important, so be there. I asked what time it would start. Four o'clock, came the answer. I had private business to attend to after seven o'clock, I said, but I would be happy to attend until then.

"What's that supposed to mean? Which is more important, official business or your private affairs? Think about it. We need you there."

The woman I had been living with for many years was about to return to the United States for a while, and, as a parting ceremony, I had arranged for us to go to an expensive French restaurant that evening. After six o'clock, it is only natural to give priority to my private affairs, I feel, and that has always been my policy. But after being admonished publicly in such a way, carrying out that policy was not easy.

It was a lucky break for me that the meeting started so early, I thought. With three hours at my disposal, I would be able to contribute significantly to the discussion, and since this was the first meeting, it would probably be over quickly anyway, I thought. Wrong again.

After six o'clock, the usual beer and snacks were brought out. The designation "free talking" was appropriate; everyone talked idly on and on about nothing in particular. A little before seven, the leader started asking people what they wanted for dinner—a clear signal that, as usual, we would be taking the last train home.

"Free talking" may sound deceptively meaningful but in fact refers to a meeting where, for the most part, people sit around and waste time doing nothing but drinking beer, chit-chatting about everything under the sun, and telling ribald stories. Missing one of these meetings does absolutely no harm; any number of free-talking sessions are held in all, and in the beginning not even the section head bothers to come.

I had been told I was an important member of the committee, and it often happens that important committee members miss a session or two. For some reason, they were being especially hard on me. At the least little thing, I became a target of *ijime*, mass teasing or bullying. I knew that if I explained the situation to this deputy, who was always forcing me to make sacrifices in the name of *tatemae*, he would only scowl and then mock me in front of everyone.

Any group exerts a force that has a powerful ability to control behavior—all the more so when everyone is keeping a sharp watch on you. It was not going to be easy getting out of the room, I could tell. In between spurts of "free talking," I plotted my escape. Having assumed I would be home before seven, I of course had not told her that I would be late. I thought of calling the restaurant to change our reservation to a later hour, but from the way things were going, the meeting showed no sign of ending before ten. This was to be our farewell date. How could I tell her I had to cancel it because of work? Especially "work" as frivolous as this.

We were scheduled to meet in the restaurant at seven-thirty. I began to panic. But the human brain is a marvelous thing; it comes through, under pressure, with good ideas. I had my plan: all I needed to do was excuse myself on the pretext of going to the men's room and then head straight for the restaurant.

"Excuse me, I'm going to the men's room," I said. Just as I expected, no one tried to stop me, and I hurried to the elevator. Then it occurred to me that if anyone spotted me there I would be doomed, so I climbed the emergency stairs to the eleventh floor and then took the elevator nonstop to the first floor. To avoid being seen by any of my co-workers, I avoided the main entranceway and fled out the back. Fortunately, a taxi pulled up just as I emerged, and I climbed in and took off straight for the restaurant.

My plans for a leisurely, uninterrupted meal, however, were not to be realized. At about ten-thirty, the manager of the restaurant told me I was wanted on the telephone. Wondering who could it be, since no one knew where I was, I picked up the phone. The chairman of the meeting said, "Miyamoto, everybody's furious. You'd better prepare yourself." Then he hung up.

Visions of what horrible fate might await me the following day at work flew around in my head, but there was no point in dwelling on that now. Tomorrow was another day, I thought, and decided to go back to concentrating on my dinner.

After going home, I tried to puzzle out how they could have found me. Then I remembered that a few days before, I had happened to mention to one of my co-workers that I would be going to the restaurant. The guy must have ratted on me. From that time on, I lost the ability to trust those around me and developed an automatic suspicion of even people who seemed to be on my side. The experience was graphic proof of the powerful influence of environment on human psychology.

Which Is More Important, Work or Private Affairs?

The next day I was at work earlier than usual and discovered that a set of bedding usually stored away somewhere was spread out on the floor by the sofa. A few of the men had evidently spent the night at the Ministry of Health and Welfare Hotel. How on earth had that come about, I inquired.

"Well, when you disappeared, there was a huge commotion. The meeting broke down. Then the senior deputy went wild and starting guzzling whisky, so the younger guys were elected to stay and keep him company."

Having been told to prepare myself, I assumed there would be some sort of response to what had happened and spent the whole day in a state of anticipation, but no one said anything. There was, however, a strange tension in the air. Everyone treated me distantly. This was the quiet before the storm, I thought. Sure enough, three days later, the storm broke.

The senior deputy, who had been drinking, came up to me and said, "What the hell do you think you're doing, ditching an important meeting like that? You occupy a responsible position in government service, you know. What are you trying to do, corrupt discipline around here?"

He then dragged out the time I had gone overseas on my vacation, trying his best to be irritating. "Not only that, what about that trip overseas you took before? You never said a word to me about it. Why not?"

"I don't see any point in digging up that issue again. It's all been settled."

"I just don't like your attitude. If you're going off some-where, why don't you come out and say so?"

"I did. I told you I had private business to attend to. You wouldn't listen."

"Have you forgotten that I asked you which was more important, your private business or your work?"

"I remember. But from what I hear, that meeting really didn't amount to much."

"The content of the meeting doesn't matter. The point is, you took off in the middle of it."

"Last night, my private affairs had priority over work."

"I've never heard such bullshit. Work has priority over everything."

"To you it does. My approach is more flexible," I said, using the English word.

"*Fureki*... huh? This is Japan—speak Japanese."

I restated the idea without using loanwords from English. "I mean, I adapt to circumstances. When I have an important meeting, I'll make sacrifices to attend it, if I have to. But a casual get-together like yesterday's is hardly worth sacrificing my personal life for."

"You haven't got the proper spirit for a civil servant. I ought to teach you a thing or two."

"That won't be necessary. I am perfectly capable of judging for myself what is important and what's not."

"Oh, yeah? What about that vacation you took? You should have told me what you were going to do."

"I had the approval of the director and the director general, so I didn't think I needed your okay."

"You can't just ignore me. If you'd come to me, I sure as hell wouldn't have let you go on any trip abroad."

"You have no right to restrict my actions. It's my right to take a vacation. Besides, my vacation has nothing to do with the fact that I slipped out of the free-talking session."

"You've really got an attitude, you know that?"

"I'm sorry, but I can't change. And I'm not here to please you, anyway. Just do me a favor and don't interfere with my personal life."

"After all this time, you still can't get America out of your system, can you? Let me set you straight about things. Sit down over there and I'll give you a good talking-to."

"Neither you nor anyone else is going to change my principles. It's a waste of time, so forget it. You'd better realize who you're up against."

"Why you little . . ."

At this point some co-workers who overheard broke in.

This exchange led to another scene the next morning. As soon as the director came in, he ordered me to come with him to the office of the director general, where I was made to apologize for the previous night. Apparently, my response to the senior deputy had broken the unwritten law against disturbing the harmony of the group. Seems like I always get left holding the bag.

Budget Realities

Back to "free talking." Free talking is the first step in working out the content of the budget plan for the following year. It goes on for a couple of months, during which priorities gradually take shape. My participation in free-talking sessions taught me some budget realities.

Until then, I had always thought that the budget was a request made to the Ministry of Finance after planning long-term visions—twenty to fifty years—and calculating what it would cost. In fact, I realized, immediate considerations carry far more weight: what receives greatest play in the media and what stands to earn popular favor were what the bureaucrats had in mind as they planned their new budgets.

The village mentality of the bureaucracy is what lies behind such a response. The government bureaucracy, Japan's largest organization, is really an aggregate of numerous smaller units—section, department, bureau—that are like so many villages. Inter-village competition, which is fierce, centers on which village will be able to expand. The clearest demonstration of an expansion of power is a budget increase, which also enhances the prestige of the ranking official. Engineering a budget hike thus becomes a primary concern, and it can happen that projects for the new year are thought up in a hit-or-miss, haphazard way.

New undertakings are first conceived in the department that will be responsible for carrying them out. Plans must go through the bureau and the accounting department before being presented to the Ministry of Finance for assessment. Naturally, many people become involved along the way. The more people whose approval is necessary for a plan, the more opinions there are offered on it—and, because bureaucracies have a vested interest in preserving the status quo, everyone's opinions get boiled down together and worked into the final product. As a result, no plan marking a significant break with established ways of thinking has the slightest chance of seeing the light of day.

The bureaucracy is constructed on an accumulation of established projects; anyone with influence on these projects maintains great administrative authority. Budgets, however, have fixed upper limits known as ceilings, so that no new project can be approved unless some other, established project is done away with. To do away with an established project means narrowing one's vested authority; naturally, this rarely happens. Any executive who allowed his authority to be narrowed would be automatically disqualified from his post.

Social Urgency and Gaiatsu, Outside Pressure

When pushing for a new project in such a conservative environment, the phrase "social urgency" becomes a persuasive tool. That is all the more reason why attention tends to be drawn to whatever is making a splash in the national media.

Officials sometimes use the internal dynamics of the ministries to their own advantage, making sure that their pet plans are taken up by the media. The reason that new administrative policies of the government appear in the newspapers in July and August is that powerful officials, usually department directors, leak news to the media. Since summer is a slow time for news, the media are all too glad to become indebted in this way and become willing boosters of the administration.

Once a plan has been taken up in the newspapers and elsewhere and people are talking about it, an argument for social urgency can be made, and those doing all in their power to trim the budget are forced to back off.

Other issues that are easily translated into budget items are those causing a stir in society as a whole, and those that arouse people's sympathy and/or tug at their emotions. The fastest way to secure control of the budget, in other words, is to enter the world of sentimentality.

Not long after I joined the Ministry of Health and Welfare, a young official gave me this advice: "Dr. Miyamoto, if you want to pursue some policy that requires a shift in thinking, or gain control of the budget for some new project, the best thing to do is to use *gaiatsu*, foreign pressure. That's the smart way. It's especially effective if you can manipulate international organizations like WHO."

Yes, of course, I thought, to exploit the Japanese weakness in the face of outside pressure makes certain sense. Even if you ended up overturning the work of some antiquated senior official, it would be easy to deflect criticism. "But doesn't an approach like that lack independence?" I asked and was blithely told, "What difference does that make? This way, I get to carry out my pet project, no one is hurt, and everybody's happy." Listening, I recalled the comment made by a seventeen-year-old girl taken into protective custody by police for acts of prostitution. "My customers feel good, and I get pocket money. Everybody's happy, officer, so what's the harm?"

It is a fact that in the ministries, budget appropriations are made not on the basis of requests built on well-thought-out policies, but on hit-or-miss petitions of easy virtue. "Can't help it, old boy, *gaiatsu,* you know": with such a reason to back you up, no one can complain. As long as foreign countries are made the villains, insiders—residents of the government "village"—can get along without altercations. Thus, the village peace is preserved.

I can't help wondering, though, if pleading foreign pressure as an excuse to preserve the village peace is an act worthy of a full-fledged member of the international community.

Pathways to Power

Given all this, free-talking sessions are in essence meetings to decide the quickest way to wrest money from the Ministry of Finance. Let me add that, unlikely as it may seem, they can also produce good ideas. But for the most part, what emerges are proposals as ephemeral as the latest fashion, forgotten in two or three years. Insight and foresight are valued less than the ability to write sentences with strong emotional appeal. Straight-shooting administrators who speak out responsibly on the conduct of state affairs with consistent policies in mind tend gradually to be excluded from the pathways to power.

There is another reason why it's hard to actualize new programs based on a thoughtful assessment of future needs: within the bureaucracy, elimination of any practice, even one that is clearly behind the times, is next to impossible. Perhaps the following exchange at a meeting I once attended will help explain why.

The meeting was so tedious, and those present getting so little out of it, that I suggested to the chairman, "Starting next year, why not abolish dull meetings like this where all we do is read materials aloud, and just mail the materials to everybody instead?"

He answered, "I know, I think it's boring, too, but we can't do that. After all, there's a chunk of the budget earmarked for honoraria and transportation fees. Besides, people in outlying areas look forward to the chance to get to Tokyo once in a while."

"You mean that once something is provided for in the budget, you can't stop doing it? Why not?"

"In the government offices, as long as a certain amount of money has been budgeted for a certain purpose, it has to be used up."

"Surely it wouldn't matter if there was a little left over."

"It's not that easy. Returning unused money is taboo."

"Why is that?"

"Leftover money gives the Finance Ministry the impression that the project in question is not very important, which makes it a target of budget cuts the following year. The loss of even a single project means a smaller budget for the whole department. The director is going to take a dim view of that, since it affects his career prospects."

"But as time moves on, surely some projects become unnecessary," I said. "Wouldn't it be a far better use of the taxpayers' money to spend those funds elsewhere? Besides, if the director decides that some undertakings are outdated and should be eliminated, he's making an important administrative decision— which is what administrators are hired for, presumably. I can see how a director who decided to eliminate unnecessary meetings and save money might be praised; what I can't imagine is how it could possibly hurt his career."

"What you say makes perfect sense, but the sensible way doesn't always prevail here. For a director, allowing another department's budget to be increased at the expense of his own is a serious matter, one calling his ability into question. You'll understand after you get more used to things."

Embodiments of the Status Quo

One of the basic tenets of government bureaucracy is that the person in charge of every village (department) must, at the very least, preserve the status quo. The departmental budget is not to be reduced. That's why a director who shrinks his domain puts himself in line for a demotion. I once had occasion to talk with a retired government executive about it.

"Mr. Miyamoto, what was it like in the local medical affairs bureau where you used to be?" he asked me.

"Boring. The work itself was basically uninteresting."

"What? Bored by your work? Give me a break. The role of a government official is to see how much new work he can find at his assigned post."

"I have my day-to-day duties, but finding new work to do is almost impossible."

"It's because you go around saying things like that that people say you're not suited for government work."

"If you ask me, abolishing the local medical affairs bureau would do a lot to activate the national hospitals. The whole place is crying out for a full-scale, systematic overhaul. And if I may go a step further, nine-tenths of the national hospitals ought to be privatized if we cared about doing the right thing. Then they wouldn't be dominated by that antiquated union."

"Nonsense. What are you talking about? The national hospitals are state property. That you could even think of selling them off to the private sector proves you don't know the first thing about government service. Besides, that's the provenance of the director general, and you're a deputy director. You need to keep clearly in mind what your own job entails. That's lesson one. All you have to worry about is how to enlarge your section by bringing in more work for it to do."

"But practically speaking, over time some sections surely become outmoded and unnecessary."

"Anyone who went around talking the way you do would wind up a victim of administrative reform."

This conversation clearly shows the defensive mentality of the government official.

A more common-sensical stance toward government projects should include the disbandment of project teams after the project winds up. Plans for a new project would then begin. But in the bureaucratic world, common sense doesn't always apply.

There are still other reasons for the difficulty in effecting any change in ongoing programs. In a hierarchical society, the worst thing anyone can do is sever his relations with the people above him by criticizing them. In general, drastically altering a policy initiated by your senior, even one that has been outmoded in the natural course of events, is considered unfitting behavior for an administrative official.

Not long after my transfer to the Ministry of Defense, for example, a meeting was held to discuss the official policy regarding Acquired Immune Deficiency Syndrome (AIDS). At the time, it was the policy of the Ministry of Health and Welfare to give priority to protection of the rights of AIDS victims, and my predecessor had organized opinion within the Ministry of Defense in that direction.

Having recently returned from the United States, where I had been profoundly shaken up by the horrors of AIDS, I announced a shift in policy: along with protecting the rights of AIDS patients, I explained, we needed to take steps toward prevention and stress the dangers of AIDS. One of the defense officials then had this to say:

"Miyamoto, this is quite a different approach from that of your predecessor. If we go around trying to persuade everyone what a terrible disease this is, the rights of AIDS patients will be violated. Isn't that what the Ministry of Health and Welfare is concerned about?"

"I am well aware of the importance of the rights of AIDS patients," I replied. "But what about those people who have not yet been infected with the AIDS virus? They have a right to know about the danger of the virus. It seems to me vital in an environment like that of the Self-Defense Forces, where you have large numbers of young men crowded in together, to pound home the terrors of the disease."

"We can't have the policy changing every time someone new is put in charge," he said. "Continuation of policy is very important for civil servants. Frankly, this sort of about-face causes problems." Everyone else present supported this view, and my proposal was killed. For a government bureaucrat, straying from the path of one's predecessor has grave consequences.

Getting Approval

The process of drafting a new budget stimulates the forming of new policies. However, in the process of working out plans, it often happens that people allow emotion to prevail over questions of content. Let me give a specific example. In my division, Director H always comes up with a plan that shows far-sightedness and perspicacity. He himself also enjoys a fair amount of popularity. He does, however, have a tendency to point out the flaws in other people's thinking in a very blunt and straightforward way. Naturally, he is dogged about reform. Anyone who crosses swords with him generally loses heart and ends up going along with his reform proposal.

However, the ministry uses a parliamentary (i.e., unanimity-driven) system of approval for adopting new plans. Unanimous approval, moreover, is seen as a way to preserve harmony (*wa*). Respect for unanimity is what gets new plans into the hands of the director general. Those who allow themselves to be swayed more by emotion than by rational considerations therefore have to recruit others to ensure that approval is denied.

One night over drinks after the director left, some of my colleagues shared some of their real feelings toward the boss. A Mr. K said to me, "Miyamoto, you're the deputy director, right? It's your job to keep him from going overboard."

"His proposal looks pretty good to me."

"What do you mean? You know a lot of people are against it, don't you? The guy's got ability, I'll grant you that, but there's just something about him I don't like."

"Just because there's opposition, even a lot of it, is no reason to stop him. Besides, whether or not you like him as a person has nothing to do with the merits of his plan."

"Maybe not, but in Japan, success for a plan requires popularity. Why do you think there's so much opposition in his case? It's because nobody likes the guy. If people don't like you, you won't get far."

"Give it up, K," said another colleague. "Miyamoto spent too long in America. He doesn't get it."

"Yeah," chimed in A, "but Miyamoto himself will be director some day. He needs to know how the ministry really works. Besides, when the time comes, if he tries to push things through at his pace, he'll fare even worse than the present director.

He also needs to know that when the director starts to get carried away, it's the deputy director's job to hold him back. That's one of the deputy director's most important jobs."

"If you can't persuade the opposition," said N, "the plan won't make it. I never liked it myself. If it doesn't get final approval, it's dead."

"But it passed easily in our division," I said.

"Yours isn't the only division," A shot back. "*Nemawashi* works the other way too, you know—to *prevent* a plan from passing."

The bureaucracy is a bottom-up system. No plan—no matter how superb or beneficial to the public—has the slightest chance without the support of your colleagues.

Precedent

I'm digressing from the topic of the budget, but let me give another example of the general distaste for reform.

By my third year in the ministry, I realized that people spend enormous energy on struggling not to deviate from precedent. I became more and more exasperated with the resulting perpetual support for the status quo. Once, on my own authority, I incinerated all paperwork that I deemed unnecessary. If no documents from the past existed, I was home free, I reasoned. I'd be able to state my opinion freely, without worrying about the weight of the past.

When the question "What's been done in the past?" invariably came up, I replied, "There doesn't seem to be any relevant materials, so I'm afraid I can't say."

"What?" came the incredulous response. "That's impossible. Look again."

"I've looked everywhere," I insisted. "There just isn't anything."

Some of my superiors began sifting through mountains of

paper themselves. I couldn't very well tell them they were wasting their time, as I had incinerated what they were looking for; they would have blown their stacks. So I let it go.

"What on earth could have happened? Call your predecessor and ask him," I was told.

In the end, however, the director issued an administrative directive unbound by considerations of the past. I suspect he was well ahead of his time.

The repercussions of this incident followed me even after I'd been transferred elsewhere. Time and again, the phone would ring and it would be my frantic successor, wanting to know what had happened to some set of past materials. He even asked about things from ages ago that just didn't matter any more.

Finally I said, "Look, I burned all the old papers. The fact that you don't have anything to rely on gives you a chance now to make decisions for yourself. You can show off your administrative skills to the full. So go for it, and thank your lucky stars." I could practically feel the look of profound shock on his face coming over the telephone wires. Apparently, he told the director general about the incineration. A few days later he called back to deliver a warning.

"The director general is very upset about it, and he's furious with you. You'd better prepare yourself for the worst."

"No matter how angry he gets, those papers are gone, and nothing can bring them back. Tell him I take full responsibility." My voice may have sounded full of confidence, but I will admit that I spent the next week or two shaking in my shoes, expecting any minute to be called in. Actually, I never heard anything about it again. That was more than three years ago. I have written about the incident here in hopes that the statute of limitations will have expired by now.

And yet I'm still proud of having burned those papers. After all, in so doing I gave many people the gift of being able to make their own judgments without concern for precedent—a real rarity in the bureaucracy.

Compromise, Compromise

Let me briefly explain the budget calendar for the Ministry of Health and Welfare. Early in July, each division finalizes its request and submits it to the bureau. The overall draft budget comes to the accounting section in early August. By the end of August, the ministry is required to submit an estimate of its needs for the next fiscal year to the Ministry of Finance. Everybody follows this schedule.

During this time, what most preoccupies management is not how to draw up a sound proposal or how to sell people on the merits of their plan, but how to placate disappointed factions in each branch of the ministry. A single proposal affects many branches. Since there is a finite budget ceiling, some of the branches, inevitably, will suffer cutbacks. Those threatened with cutbacks are of course far from pleased. The adjustment process centers on efforts to assuage this discontent, and meeting after meeting is held to work out endless compromises.

Such meetings are sometimes held in the ministry; other times they may be conducted at night over a friendly glass of beer or *saké*. August, as a result, is a busy time in the ministry, hardly a time when large numbers of bureaucrats can take a leisurely vacation. Once the draft budget is in, however, there is a short breathing spell.

Party Time

One of the most important events in the bureaucracy, usually around December 20, is the unofficial budget preview from the Ministry of Finance. When it comes, some of the younger bureaucrats go around looking ecstatic. Since the announcement signals the start of a budget-share struggle called "revived negotiations," it would seem appropriate for everyone to hunker down and get serious. But in fact the opposite occurs; it's more like a big, festive party. The final seven or eight days of the year—spent around the clock in the government offices finishing up the year's business—are for many people a delightful entertainment. Imagine something like an elementary school's summer camp, held in December in the heart of the city.

Pots and pans are brought in, and everybody cooks meals together. When the day's work is done, at night the office is transformed into a big eatery, with a variety of foods laid out for the choosing—*oden* stew, riceballs, sushi, boxed lunches, sandwiches.

This is also the period when groups of lobbyists representing various affiliated groups and corporations come by. With thirty to forty guests a day, looking after them all is a big job. Fortunately for the staff, however, they always leave generous contributions of brandy, whiskey, *saké*, sweets, or other goodies (bureaucrats often put on a few pounds at this time of year). But one thing about the lobbyists makes me feel a little sorry for them: their presence or absence has no effect whatever on the final budget. Their trips are a complete waste of time, their gifts a waste of money. Someone should tell them to stay home. But this too is an annual event seemingly exempt from normal cost-benefit considerations.

Camping In

During the day, corridors are heaped high with mountains of futon bedding which will, come night, cover the floors wall to wall. The offices, never spacious to begin with, are packed so full there is barely room to pick your way through.

The solidarity that arises under these circumstances,

however, is considered irreplaceable. This camp-in is the quin-
tessence of the bureaucratic experience. When the revised
negotiations are over, I total up how many nights I have spent at
work—another litmus test, like coming to work on Sundays, to
show the strength of your commitment.

When I first came to the ministry, I kept being urged to stay
overnight with everybody else. Once, even though I had plenty
of time to get home, I decided to do so as an educational experience. I wanted to see their reaction.

The next day, I clearly remember that a large number of
my colleagues came up to me, beaming with approval, saying
things like, "Well, well, Miyamoto, I see you finally spent the
night!" Why I had stayed—the kind of work I got done—
mattered far less to them than the simple fact of my sharing
in the office camp-in. Clearly, for them it bordered on a
religious experience.

Revived Negotiations

The party goes on until the end of the revised negotiations
which involve the budget director, the director general, vice-
minister, and minister. The revised negotiations, of course, are
a mere ritual. In reality, budget revisions are based on the rank
of the officials doing the applying, with the necessary funds set
aside all along. When people of that rank come bowing and
scraping, hat in hand, it simply won't do to send them away
empty-handed. Then when they come away bearing their
trophy, they are able to create the impression that they have
accomplished some great work.

Occasionally, of course, the influence of a politician proves
necessary to revive the talks, but only in a small percentage of
cases. "None of the highest-ranking bureaucrats could succeed
in negotiating with the finance minister, but the moment a
politician steps in, the talks are revived. Those politicians really

know their stuff!" This is the impression they are able to leave with the public.

In reality, the content of the final draft is known practically from the start. I have often thought that the annual budget ritual takes place only as a way of allowing the high officials in charge of running Japan, Inc., to have their bit of time in the limelight. Since the outcome is known before they ever get started, it seems to me they'd do better to scrap such pretentiousness, but the high value placed on custom and tradition dictates otherwise. The existence of this ritual is known to every bureaucrat in Tokyo, to the press, and of course to the politicians involved. The only ones who know nothing about it are the Japanese citizens.

If people in the Finance Ministry should read this, I have no doubt they would argue that the revived negotiations are not an empty ritual at all, but that they are carried out based on accurate assessments of the situation. That is the *tatemae*, or illusion—but the *honne*, the reality, is something else.

CHAPTER

4

Japan:
A Bureaucrat's
Paradise?

The Quest for a Two-Week Vacation

"You can't be serious. You're really asking for two weeks' vacation? It looks as if you stayed so long in the United States that you're having trouble readjusting to Japan. You don't realize the responsibilities of a Japanese civil servant. Keep in mind that here, you're among the elite. My predecessor went too easy on you. I'll teach you the proper way for a civil servant to behave. Believe me, the deputy director of a section can't take more than three days of vacation in a row. Look around you. Do you see anybody who takes fourteen days off? I myself haven't had a single day off in the last ten years!"

Such was the response to my vacation request several years ago, when I worked in the Defense Agency on loan from the Ministry of Health and Welfare.

Stressing the importance of "internationalization," or fitting in with other industrialized countries, and ever mindful of foreign criticism of Japanese workaholism, the government had just grandly declared its intention of making Japan a "lifestyle superpower." The bureaucratic world in Japan is a microcosm of society at large; the actual working conditions of government officials like me, however, were (and are) a far cry from any such utopia. Having become a part of that world after a dozen years in the United States, I found myself caught between two cultures.

What perplexed me most was what to do about vacations. In the United States, employee vacations are incorporated into yearly planning, and, barring some great emergency, can usually be taken as scheduled. Those taking trips overseas, especially, need to plan a good three to five months in advance to be sure of reservations in the restaurants and hotels of their choice. But in Japan, I found, customs are far different.

Farewell Fanfare

I was surprised to find that in Japan, overseas business trips are still looked on as something special. When someone goes overseas on business, the whole section comes together for a send-off party, and the traveler receives a small going-away gift of money, in line with traditional custom. But in this age when information circuits the globe in seconds and a person can be halfway around the world in twelve hours, it is a strange anachronism for people in Japan to draw out such farewells as if they expected never to see each other again.

There is apparently a strong view that any bureaucrat going overseas is getting away with something by escaping the daily grind and is enjoying himself or herself at government expense. People are unable to accept overseas travel as a normal part of business. For many, the very word "overseas" conjures up fantasies of a life of ease and luxury. Of course, the strong allure of life overseas only points up the deep discontent many Japanese feel with their lives.

Hanging around working late night after night, surrounded by colleagues you have no real desire to be with, eating bad food—who would ask for such a life? Once you become part of a large organization, individual inclination goes out the window. The unspoken rules of the organization, distasteful as they may be to everyone, hold sway. So it is understandable that a person traveling overseas would be glad of the chance to breathe easy for a change—and no less understandable that those left behind would be envious.

In order to dispel the impression of going off to enjoy the good life, Japanese business travelers customarily schedule overseas trips on the weekend. The moment they arrive, moreover, they plunge into grueling rounds of meetings and negotiations without allotting any time for rest. Japanese participants in international conferences are well known for smiling, remaining silent, and sleeping (the so-called three Ss); of these, the last, anyway, may be safely attributed to the hectic pace of their schedules.

Overseas Travel Permits

Since even overseas business travel stirs such strong emotions among Japanese bureaucrats, taking vacations overseas simply isn't done. To do so would mean stirring up the envy of one's co-workers. Additionally, ministry regulations require anyone traveling overseas on vacation to submit two separate documents: one requesting permission to take a vacation, the other permission to travel abroad. Every time I fill out the latter document, I ask myself why on earth such a practice goes on. I once asked my director why the extra paperwork was necessary.

"Well," he replied, "that's undoubtedly because of the inconvenience caused if someone were needed at work and turned out to be someplace inaccessible overseas."

"But nowadays it's possible to go halfway around the world in a matter of hours," I protested. "Even in Japan, there are plenty of places that many hours from Tokyo."

"That's true. Well, it's only a formality, you know. I wouldn't get too upset if I were you. They rubber-stamp them except for the most extreme cases."

What he meant was "as long as you don't overstep the bounds of group-sanctioned tradition." Wondering what the situation was in other ministries, I described Health and Welfare Ministry vacation regulations to the leader of another, more liberal agency and was informed such regulations were unconstitutional. Though the man was an administrative official, he had devoted most of his life to legal interpretation and legislation. When I pressed him for an explanation, he said that such regulations contravened the right to freedom of movement. That made sense to me and convinced me that others in the Ministry of Health and Welfare might well share my way of thinking.

Wondering if anyone from my ministry had ever traveled overseas without going through the proper protocol, I looked into it but found nothing. Still, as I thought about it, I realized that it would be perfectly possible to travel overseas unbeknownst to the ministry, without filing the necessary documents. In fact, at the Defense Agency, where I was temporarily assigned, a friend of mine confessed that he had once done just that, to save time and trouble. The Ministry of Health and Welfare has the same organizational structure as the Defense Agency, and I felt there was a good chance that someone had done the same thing there as well, without ever being discovered.

Path-breaker

I had had enough of sneaking around, however, so I decided to become the first person at my ministry ever to take a trip overseas without submitting a formal request for permission to do so. I was by then director of quarantine, Port of Tokyo. Having received a request to speak on the topic of "Correlations Between Japanese Customs and Structural Impediments," I was scheduled to visit Washington, D.C., to give the speech. I decided to use my vacation time for the occasion, just to see what response the ministry legal experts would come up with and to learn what I was up against.

The ordinary form for requesting a vacation has a space for indicating the reason for the time off; nine times out of ten, people write "personal affairs." I, however, boldly put down "to deliver an address in Washington, D.C." Government officials have a tendency to apply the rules they make to suit their own convenience. The system tends to ignore people who, like me, speak out publicly and bluntly against customary practices. By that I mean that we are simply not taken seriously. Had I informed my supervisor orally of my intention to go to Washington, D.C., to deliver an address, he would in all likelihood not have batted an eyelash.

To bring matters to a head and force those in authority to deal with me on my own terms, I deliberately chose to write out the actual reason for my trip on the vacation request form. Bureaucratic regard for protocol would, I reasoned, force authorities to insist that I submit a request for overseas travel. Then I would be able to see for myself how the situation sized up.

Sure enough, I received repeated reminders to submit the missing document. There was even a standard bureaucratic warning: "Failure to submit the prescribed petition is a violation of official regulations." I told my supervisor to go ahead and punish me for violating the rules if he wished, adding that if he did, I would sue on grounds that the rules were a violation of my constitutional rights. In the end I took off for Washington without ever having submitted the request for permission to travel overseas.

Ex Post Facto Compliance

On my return after a week-long trip, my supervisor pleaded with me to go ahead and submit the form after the fact, assuring me that it still wasn't too late. I had no grudge against him and regretted the trouble I was causing him, but still I felt unable to give in on a matter of principle.

I took him out for lunch and explained, "I have nothing against you personally; I am simply trying to do away with fusty, anachronistic customs in the organization." He seemed half persuaded that I was right and half convinced that I was a crackpot.

"Personally," he told me, "it's all the same to me whether you turn in the form or not. But it's my job to get one from you, and as long as I don't, I'll catch hell from my boss. That's the only reason I keep after you about it."

To win him over, I explained, "Actually, no matter how you look at it, the system is weird. It puts priority on the needs of the organization and restricts personal freedom. I'd like to see the system gradually abolished or rendered obsolete. To do that, I need to establish a precedent, since precedents are what count around here. If I succeed, other people will be able to travel overseas freely, without any stigma attached to them. That's my main objective."

Whether I convinced him or not I cannot say, but after that he stopped giving me such a hard time. Instead, his immediate superior, the director general, began coaxing me in honeyed tones to turn in the missing document. This was a man I had once locked horns with in a debate concerning long vacations. Even though I had submitted all the necessary paperwork for a vacation, I'd been accused of failure to do so and slapped with a punishment for being absent without leave. Ex post facto submission of all sorts of documents is common in the ministry, but I was informed then that in my case, no such permission could be granted.

"You've done a complete about-face, haven't you?" I said. "Last time you refused to let me submit a vacation request form after the fact, on the grounds that no special exceptions were allowed. Now you are urging me to do that very thing. Quite a contradiction, wouldn't you say?"

With a sheepish look, he said, "I don't want to have to bother personnel about you anymore, Miyamoto," and urged me to go ahead and submit the overseas travel request.

The tug of war went on another month or so, but I never did submit the requested document. Nor did the head of personnel ever formally declare me in violation of ministry regulations, perhaps to keep the whole affair from escalating still further.

Later on, an administrator confessed to me that had I simply written down "personal reasons" in the appropriate space, they would willingly have extended tacit permission for my trip abroad; my open declaration of plans to deliver an address in Washington, D.C., effectively tied their hands. To make matters worse, I was a past offender who had once been disciplined for ignoring customary procedure at the ministry. My apparent failure to reflect on the errors of my ways had made them indignant, he said. Even so, having never intended to get tough in the first place, and for all I know fearing that they themselves would be the ones to suffer from adverse publicity, they did in the end grant me tacit permission. Evidently my friend from the other ministry had been correct in his reading of the situation.

I, however, was satisfied with what I had achieved. In

traveling abroad without an official permit while escaping official censure, I had succeeded in establishing a precedent—my very intention all along.

"There's No Precedent"

Let me explain the procedure involved in taking a vacation. Final approval for a travel request is given by the director general, but before he ever sees the documents, they must be stamped by the applicant's immediate supervisor, as well as by the deputy director, the chief deputy director, and the chief. As a result, it often happens that a request hits a snag before reaching the director general's desk. And although the director general has final say over issues relating to usual practice, in point of fact it is one's peers who control the situation.

Above all, you have to take pains to ensure that none of your colleagues comments on the lack of a precedent. Most bureaucrats believe in preserving the status quo and use complaints about lack of precedent as grounds for doing so. To protest that something has never been done before is an effective way to keep matters from moving forward and ensure that ministry operations stay on hold. The organization exerts an invisible power on its members, moving them to grumble about precedents in order to ensure the perpetuity of long-standing customs.

Thus the cry "It's never been done before!" has a powerful influence. My organization has established a system that blocks a request for a long vacation *if even one person objects.* Vacations are a personal right, but if one person takes a long vacation, it is assumed that office harmony will be disrupted.

Some of my supervisors are sympathetic. One assured me that he had no objection to my taking a vacation, as long as I made no waves in the process. He urged me to consult with my colleagues in advance, to gain their understanding and approval. He certainly meant well by the suggestion, and at the time I accepted it gratefully, but the more I thought about what he had said, the stranger it seemed. If it is my right to take a vacation, why should exercising that right be likely to make waves?

The system is set up in such a way, of course, that as long as correct procedure is followed, no one, not even the director general, can flatly turn down a request for overseas travel. In that case, however, the traveler would arouse strong envy in his colleagues and antagonize his superiors at the same time, so anyone undertaking such a step must be prepared to renounce all career ambitions in the bureaucracy. In other words, in the Japanese government, choosing to exercise a natural right can lead to ostracism if the group withholds its approval. To insist on one's rights in such an environment requires tremendous courage and exacts a stiff price.

The Ultimate Excuse

In any case I went ahead and planned a two-week vacation in Italy and France for the summer. But how to convince my supervisor of the need for a trip? Since, at the time, I still had dreams of advancement in my career, the truth would hardly do.

After a great deal of thought, I came up with a plausible story: I decided to tell my director that I had to attend Buddhist memorial services in Wakayama Prefecture. This would carry considerable weight, given the bureaucratic mentality that attaches great importance to ceremonial events such as weddings and funerals. (Attending funerals, in particular, is even considered part of one's work duties.) Even so, asking for two weeks off to attend a one-day memorial service was a bit much. My plan would have to be refined.

And so I trotted out my aged, ailing mother. For Mother, I

explained, these services represented what might well be her last chance to visit relatives. And since there was no one else in the immediate family, I had no choice but to go along and look after her on the trip.

I chose Wakayama Prefecture for two reasons: first, it happens to be my birthplace; second, even by bullet train, it is a good twelve hours from Tokyo. My mother's frail condition would make long train travel impossible, necessitating an overnight stay in Osaka. In order for her to see relatives not attending the memorial services, I decided to have us make the rounds of family members in other cities all over Japan. No son could have been more devoted, more dutiful than I in wanting to grant my mother's last wish. I stated my case with tears in my eyes, carefully calculating the effect.

Every year, early in June, a sheet of paper is circulated in the ministry offices on which each person indicates his or her summer vacation plans. There is, of course, a catch: everyone's vacation plans become public knowledge, and anyone asking for more time off than the rest stands out like a sore thumb. In the strict hierarchy of the Japanese bureaucratic world, taking more time off than a superior is inconceivable. If for some reason or other your vacation time will exceed that of your superiors, you try to conceal the fact as best you can by splitting your vacation into several less-conspicuous chunks. Even so, no one ever takes off more than two or three days longer than his superiors.

Right or Duty?

I went ahead and submitted my vacation request to the chief deputy director of my division, who took one look and said, "Forget it." Swiftly rebuffed, I decided to try a new ploy: toadying.

This chief deputy director typically hung around the office

after hours to drink *saké* and watch TV. One day I stayed on as well, watching the tube with him and pouring his drinks. After several rounds, I broached the matter again, and he finally yielded: "You win, Dr. Miyamoto. You came here from the Ministry of Health and Welfare and so did our director; if he approves your request, it's all right with me."

The director's initial response, when I went to see him the following day, is given at the beginning of this chapter. The rest of our conversation went along these lines:

"What's wrong with me attending memorial services for my ancestors?"

"Nothing. The problem is time. It's too damn long."

"But the end of June falls in the official summer vacation, and the chief deputy director says he has no objection."

"How can I maintain office discipline if I approve a request like this? Believe me, everyone else would like a long vacation too, but they go along with the system. I can't make special allowances just for you. Besides, your job should be keeping you pretty busy. You can't afford to take off so much time, can you?"

"If people want vacations, they should ask for them. They're all so afraid of what others will think that they can't speak their minds. If I go around worrying about people like that, I won't be able to do anything at all. If you ask me, constantly worrying about what people will think isn't good for the organization, either."

"If everyone starts taking vacations, no work will get done. Is that what you want to see happen?

"The reason nothing gets done is that people hang around the office half the night, drinking while they work. If everyone worked more efficiently, we could finish up all our work in the morning."

"Well, well. You've got all the answers, haven't you? Your trouble is, you don't really listen to what other people have to say."

"They have their way of thinking, I have mine. It's my right to take a vacation if I want to. Why should I have to go around asking other people's advice about something that's a basic right? And I have a right to a paid vacation, too."

"Rights, rights, rights. What about your duties as a civil servant? Are you fulfilling those?"

"Absolutely. All the work that needs to be done gets on your desk within the prescribed time, doesn't it?

"But there's always more work waiting to be done."

"Well, if you're going to be that way about it, no one can ever take a vacation, now can they?"

"Look, everyone can hear us. Lower your voice, will you? You and I are both here on loan from the Ministry of Health and Welfare, and we get treated as outsiders as it is. We've got to present a united front if we don't want to lose our posts."

"I don't see what that's got to do with my vacation request."

"Dr. Miyamoto, please understand my position."

"That's a very clever tactic, sir. If I say I do understand, you'll expect me to shorten my vacation, and if I say I don't, it will mean I have no common sense. Either way, you've got me."

"Your stubbornness is amazing."

"Oh? Which of us is the stubborn one? It seems to me you are closing your eyes to what people really think nowadays."

"Tell me this: Which means more to you, your work or your vacation?"

"Another trap. If I say work, you'll tell me to put up with the short vacations, won't you? Sorry, I'm not falling for it."

"But if everyone asked for vacations the way you do, work would come to a standstill!"

"Isn't it the job of an administrator to make sure that work gets done even if everyone takes off an appropriate amount of time? I hardly think a work environment that discourages people from taking vacations is something an administrator should brag about."

"There you go again, an answer for everything. You've got quite a mouth. I guess I've got no choice but to go along with you, but let me make one little change in your plans. You've asked for fourteen consecutive days off. I want you to report for work sometime in the middle, just for a morning or an afternoon. That way, your vacation will be split in two. It'll cost a bit extra in transportation, but I'm sure you can manage it."

His solution left me stunned. How was I going to pop back from Europe midway through my trip? What's more, I was fed up by his constant worrying over appearances; how to make it look good so that he could avoid blame was all the man cared about.

I said to him, "There's no way I can come back midway. If I'm not there, who's going to look after my mother?"

"With all those relatives on hand, it shouldn't matter if you're gone for a day or two," he replied.

"But by the middle of the vacation we'll have left Wakayama. I'm sorry, but I cannot accept those terms."

After four solid hours of me sticking to my guns, the director's attitude had undergone a significant but subtle change. If I didn't press my advantage home, all would be lost. I racked my brains for something to say that would cement my position.

"If you agree to this request," I said, "then I agree not to ask for any of my remaining vacation time this year." There were only eight days left anyway. I planned to let them accumulate till next year and then ask for three weeks off.

"Good God," he said. "You could hardly ask for more time off after getting two weeks' vacation! Oh, what the hell. If I tell them you've agreed to forfeit the rest of your vacation days, they'll probably swallow it."

At long last the director approved my request. As I was leaving his office, however, he casually ordered me to leave word with the chief deputy director as to where I could be reached during my absence. Great. More trouble. I could leave a relative's phone number, but what if someone actually called me up? A child might answer the telephone and say truthfully that I was nowhere around. What then? Still, sitting around imagining dire possibilities would only defeat my purpose, so I stopped worrying. If worst came to worst, I would just have to deal with the situation as best I could when the time came.

A Pathetic Philosophy of Life

I had spent all afternoon getting approval for two weeks of vacation. My persistence had paid off, but overall the amount of time wasted was enormous. I had learned, however, that zeal and determination were indispensable if I was to succeed—even with a sterling excuse like attending Buddhist memorial services for my ancestors. Had I walked in and asked permission to go on a gourmet tour of France and Italy, they would have laughed right in my face.

What amazes me is that even though I am fully entitled to a paid vacation, I have to furnish a detailed account of how I plan to spend my time. I also have to obtain the understanding and consent of so many different people that the process of explaining myself goes on and on. In fact, where and how I choose to spend my vacation is my business, and there should be no need to explain or persuade anyone of anything. It all goes to show how little respect for privacy there is in the bureaucratic world of Japan. With such anachronistic values among the top administrators of Japan, Inc., all you can say is that this country is way behind the times. Far from being a "lifestyle superpower," Japan can only be called a backward nation in this respect.

I explained the situation in detail to my relatives around the country and underscored that if by any chance someone from the ministry should call, they were to say that I was out and that I would return the call later. Then they were to telephone my mother right away. I would phone home from Europe every day to make sure all was well. With every contingency thus pro-vided for, I could at last leave the country. There was nothing left to do but pray that no one from the office would try to get in touch with me.

The first six days went smoothly. Early on the morning of the seventh day, however, I was jarred awake by a phone call from my mother. There had been a call from my office, and they wanted to reach me. What to do?

To an experienced ear, the background noise of an interna-tional call would give away the game. I decided to experiment by calling a friend in Tokyo first. Out of five calls I placed, two, he said, were clearly international, but with the other three it was virtually impossible to tell.

What the hell. Might as well go for broke, I thought, and made the call. The ministry operator instantly recognized that it was an international call, but I assured her the noise was due to my using a cordless telephone. She put me through, and it turned out that a friend of mine had telephoned the office, wanting to get in touch with me—that was all. The person I spoke to seemed unaware that I was calling from overseas. Still, it was a close shave. As I retell the story now, it may sound comi-cal, but at the time it was anything but that. I'm not proud of the fact that I lied, but I am convinced that I had no other choice in order to protect my rights.

Japanese government offices are full of middle-aged men who boast that they are *sodai gomi* (literally "large garbage"), slang for useless husbands who do nothing but take up space around the house. If they go home they are only in the way, so they feel more comfortable at work, they say unashamedly. They are proud of their lifestyle and outdo one another in bragging about how little of their allotted vacation days they have used up. Anyone who admits he wouldn't mind some time off is scowled at and treated to a dose of their sorry philosophy of life. As long as this tribe of people continues to exist, long vacations for government workers will remain an impossible dream.

Marching Lock-Step

The extreme difficulty of taking a long vacation if you work in the bureaucratic world of Japan should by now be apparent, but lots of other bureaucratic customs are equally resistant to change. The importance of marching lock-step can be seen not only in regard to vacations but in other areas as well.

Shortly after I joined the Ministry of Health and Welfare, I had the opportunity of dining, together with my colleagues and seniors, at a French restaurant with the former minister. I ordered freely from the menu, but everyone else ordered the same thing as the ex-minister. The dinner set before me was thus different from everyone else's. My failure to conform caused a small sensation. The former minister himself said nothing, but others made pointed remarks about my food, commenting drily on how good it looked, or asking me point-blank what it was. I understood they were being sarcastic, but paid no attention and only answered innocently that I was extremely fond of rabbit. The stymied looks on their faces were a sight to see.

In Japan, a government official makes no distinction between work and private life. Or, to be more precise, he sacrifices his private life for the sake of his work. Staying in the office as late as ten or eleven is considered natural. On rare days when everyone's work gets wrapped up early and he would like nothing better than to go home and relax, he is urged to go drinking with the gang. After that comes the karaoke bar; by the time it closes, he has to race to catch the last train home. On Sundays, it is group golf. The faces of his co-workers are never long out of his sight.

One day soon after my return to Japan, I received orders to help my director move to a new house the following Sunday.

This sort of request is commonplace in all the government ministries. The reason for the practice, I was informed, is to lower
moving costs. As soon as the moving job was done, however, the
director took us all out to a restaurant and spent the equivalent
of over $300 on food and drink. Any money he may have saved
on moving expenses thus went straight toward our entertainment.

A similar incident took place when one of the directors
went overseas on business. Drive him to Narita airport, I was
ordered. Having little choice in the matter, I did, in my own car,
at my own expense. Again, it was a Sunday. If someone wanted
to ingratiate himself with a superior in this manner, I might be
able to understand, but the idea that the organization could
order me to do it came as a shock.

When I later asked for time off in compensation, I was told
that, as my actions had been based on goodwill, they could not
be considered "work"; therefore, applying for any form of compensation would be unreasonable. As I see it, a system that
attempts to deny the existence of private time is far more unreasonable.

Sunday at the Office: The Ultimate Test of Loyalty

In psychoanalytic terms, the desire to remain constantly
together—the essence of bureaucratic mentality—is a sign of
insecurity. Separation triggers fear that the others may disappear permanently. Alone, most bureaucrats are incapable of
stating an opinion, but have no difficulty doing so as part of a
group. This behavior demonstrates that they attempt to establish their identities by acting in groups. And yet government
bureaucrats are responsible for Japan's actions on the world
stage vis-à-vis other countries. I am surely not alone in believing
that they should develop into strong individuals, capable of
holding their own in one-on-one situations.

I was surprised when I first went to work at the ministry to discover that my colleagues would report to the office regularly on Sundays. Willingness to do so was regarded as a significant demonstration of loyalty; conversely, failure to do so evoked considerable pressure to conform. Once the general director of my division announced loudly, "People just back from America sure have it easy! They get to spend their days off any way they want." Another time, one of my superiors told me that showing up on Sundays now and then would help advance my career—whether or not I actually did any work. The spirit of the Olympic Games seems no less applicable to Japanese ministries: participation counts more than performance.

I decided that I too would make a show of loyalty. But since it goes against my grain to waste even an hour in idiocy, I came up with a plan. For security purposes, all those showing up at the ministry on a Sunday must show their ID and sign their names in a book. There is a separate book for each division, so that anyone showing up for work the next day can tell at a glance who was in the office over the weekend. Choosing a Sunday when there was little work to do, I went to the security office in the morning and signed in. After that I went to a sports club and then I did some shopping. In the evening, I went back and signed myself out. The next day, when I went back to work, my colleagues complimented me on my newfound willingness to come in on Sunday, plainly startled but gratified by my apparent conversion. The stranger from America had finally started to think and act like a bureaucrat. They long continued in this happy misunderstanding, never suspecting my subterfuge.

"Voluntary" Overtime

Overtime work is an accepted part of life not only in government offices but throughout Japanese industry. Budget restraints, however, put effective limits on how much people can be paid for it. In the ministries, each section receives a special allotment for overtime, which the general director divvies up equally on the basis of individual workload. Such a system makes sense only if it is assumed that overtime is a normal part of one's duties.

Furthermore, overtime payments cover only one-fourth or one-fifth of the actual hours worked. The rest is unpaid, or what they call "voluntary" overtime. Labor in the bureaucracy consists of regular working hours plus overtime plus complimentary overtime. The government is thus hardly in a position to provide "administrative guidance" for the abolishment of unpaid overtime.

The Diet is another major obstacle to the Japanese bureaucrat's pursuit of personal freedom and happiness. The reason is that no clear boundary exists between the parliamentary and the bureaucratic worlds. As long as the Diet is in session, government bureaucrats have an increased workload, whether they like it or not. Not long after it became official that the ministries were to adopt a five-day workweek, I telephoned the general office of the Diet to see how this might affect parliamentary proceedings. The man who took my call offered the following explanation: "In principle, the Diet will adjourn for weekends, but we have an agreement that Diet sessions are not to be bound by the working hours of government offices."

This statement cannot be taken at face value. Practically speaking, there is no separation of powers in Japan; bureaucrats enjoy extensive lawmaking powers. They not only write most of the bills put forward in the Diet but script most of the debates that take place there as well. That is why ministry officials are forced to put in long hours while the Diet is in session. Without the support of the bureaucrats, Diet members would be unable to function. It's no exaggeration to say that the Diet is the highest power of the state in name only; in actuality, it is little more than a branch of the bureaucracy. Not until Diet members begin to draft laws on their own, without relying on bureaucrats to do it for them, will the bureaucrats be able to enjoy weekends off and drop the custom of voluntary overtime.

In response to criticism from foreign countries that Japanese people spend too much time on the job, the government began a push to remedy the situation by shortening working hours. This push culminated in the official adoption of a five-day workweek in May 1992, and the entire government took the lead in reducing employee work hours—at least on paper. Realities, however, will change only when the problem of unpaid overtime is tackled head-on. Under present conditions, work hours that show up as statistics may well be reduced, but a corresponding increase in unpaid overtime means a net change of zero. An anachronistic belief in the virtue of *messhi hoko,* sacrificing oneself for the good of the organization, prevents pernicious practices like unpaid overtime from ever being eradicated.

Government offices excel at the manipulation of statistics. Mere number-juggling, however, unaccompanied by substantive changes, cannot, in the long term, satisfy the complaints of foreign countries. Sooner or later the truth will come out. The real impetus for a reduction in workers' hours can come only when Japan switches to an emphasis on the needs of consumers, not producers, and of individuals, not companies.

In the West, a clear distinction is made between private time and work; people treasure their private time. In Japan, on the other hand, people work hard late into the night, producing goods for export. Given a workday of eight hours in the West, and one of fifteen hours in Japan, can competition be fair?

Work: "Necessary Evil" or "Good"?

Current theory in Japan has it that there is a fundamental opposition between Japanese and Western outlooks on the meaning and importance of work. In the West, it is argued, work is looked on not as something innately good but as drudgery divinely imposed on humankind as retribution for sin, freedom from which can be won only by faithfully following the teachings of God.

In Japan, by contrast, work has traditionally been seen as an act of virtue, as epitomized in the teachings of the agricultural philosopher and supposed paragon of virtue Ninomiya Sontoku (1787–1856), whose statue as a young man is familiar to elementary schoolchildren all over the country. In sum, the theory says that Western values regarding work cannot easily be transplanted to Japan.

Looked at from the perspective of human psychology, however, this theory has an essential flaw. The pursuit of happiness is part of the psychological makeup of every human being. This "pleasure principle" is a human instinct that knows no national boundaries. It is only natural that people should like pleasure, or ease, and dislike labor, or work.

In Western societies, work is generally considered a means of sustaining one's personal life and is not allowed to erode it. Then, from far-off Asia, along came Japanese companies with high-quality products for sale. Ignoring Western standards of work, they go all-out to produce and sell their products. Under these conditions, the only way for the West to stay competitive with Japan is to lengthen its working hours. Westerners therefore face the unenviable choice of either altering their core values and sacrificing their personal lives in order to compete with Japan, or sitting back in defeat and allowing their markets to be flooded with Japanese products. In either case—even if they succeed in remaining competitive, and certainly if they give up the fight altogether—they lose.

Under the circumstances, you can hardly blame Westerners for complaining angrily that Japan does not play fair. Even former French Minister of Labor Edith Cresson's radical statement that the Japanese are bent on "world conquest" cannot be dismissed as irrational or absurd.

For Japan, internationalization is a matter of crucial importance, for a variety of reasons. As long as Japan considers itself a member of the advanced nations of the West, however, it must accept and embrace Western values. It must at all cost avoid imposing its own values on the West and leading the West down a path that will result in the abandonment of anything so fundamental as the belief in the importance of an individual's right to private time.

What is the point in manufacturing quality, state-of-the-art products if no one has a comfortable, relaxed enough life to enjoy them? Japanese living conditions resemble nothing so much as a warehouse piled high with world-class products, where people smugly pat themselves on the back and brag of their fancied superiority. It ought to be the goal not only of Western society, but of every society on earth, for citizens to enjoy leisure time to be with family and friends and pursue their personal goals.

The life philosophy that sees work as a tool for the enrichment of personal life seems to me far more humane than a policy of urging people to sacrifice their personal lives for the good of the organization. This is the direction in which Japan needs to move if it is to become a true "lifestyle superpower."

The Bureaucrat as Actor

"Write Like an Adult"

The previous chapter originally appeared as an article in the June 1992 issue of the *Monthly Asahi*. At the time, I decided not to show it to top ministry officials until the galley proofs were ready. When I did so, their reaction was unanimous: "Can't you do something to stop the presses?"

One of my superiors in the Ministry of Health and Welfare scolded, "What do you mean by writing such trash? If you were going to identify people by their titles, you might at least have gotten permission first!" He wound up by inviting me to resign: "If you plan on writing about government offices, do so after you leave. When do you plan on leaving, anyway?"

Someone else had this to say: "You're young, so you write in a clear, concise, simple style. You'd better learn to write like an adult." When I asked him what he meant, he explained, "For example, choosing more abstract expressions; phrasing things so it's impossible to say whether you're writing what you yourself think, or general opinion."

I was amazed. True, what I had written may have been fairly strong stuff. My aim, however, was not to kiss and tell but to point out that if Japan was to remain a full-fledged member of the international community, there were certain internationally accepted rules that we would have to go along with. I was concerned in particular about the oft-noted fact that Japanese society compels its workers to work too hard, and I wanted to consider the causes and ramifications of overwork. It seemed to me that rather than a lot of abstract theorizing, an account of my own experiences in the government bureaucracy—a microcosm of Japanese society at large—would be more to the point. And that's what I did, in detail, without trying to cover up my own misdeeds.

Of course, I had envisaged that the article would generate a certain response within the ministries, but nothing like this. Showered with reprimands from my superiors, I couldn't help losing my nerve and regretting what I had done.

On cooler reflection, however, I was left unpersuaded by anything anyone had said. They were using a peculiarly Japanese kind of logic, one that was poorly suited to Japan's avowed goal of becoming a respected member of the community of nations. This funny logic, above all, seemed to be the greatest obstacle to Japan's "internationalization." Once that realization came to me, I became even more determined to carry on.

"You Don't Understand"

I was puzzled because my critics never attacked my article as erroneous; their main concern was that I had published it without first seeking permission. Specifically, what upset the high officials was my naming of the Defense Agency, where I had previously been assigned, along with my somewhat negative comments on the Diet system. The following exchange took place around this time between myself, the director general, and the personnel manager.

"Since you've got Sanpei Sato supplying cartoon illustrations for the article," said the director general, "it's probably too late to kill it. But at the very least, you've got to eliminate the references to the Defense Agency. And cut that part about the Diet. Consider it an order."

"Yesterday I went to the Defense Agency to talk to the legal secretary there about my manuscript," I replied.

"What did he say?" the personnel manager asked.

"He said it would cause problems and asked me not to go through with it."

"I'll bet he did."

"But when I told him it was ready for press," I continued, "he sighed and accepted the situation. He didn't say a word about cutting all references to the Defense Agency."

"He didn't have anything else to say?" asked the director general.

"He said that instead of writing things like this, I'd be better off applying myself to my regular work."

"That's for sure," the personnel director chimed in.

"How I use my free time is my own affair."

"Don't fool yourself, Dr. Miyamoto," the director general replied. "You are a civil servant, and a government administrator to boot. You've got to keep in mind that people pay great attention to what you say."

"Is that really true?" I asked. "Let's be honest with each other. I know very well I was sent to the Quarantine Office because I don't follow the unwritten laws around here. I take too many days off, I don't stay after hours with everybody else, and so on. None of that is any secret. So why should anyone care what I say or do?"

"You don't understand how things work," he said. "Anyway, you've got to be more discreet. Try again to persuade the publishers to drop it."

"I'm pretty sure it's too late, but if you want me to, sir, I'll try."

"You can make the call from here," he said.

"Do the Right Thing: Save Face"

All I had done, concerning both the Defense Agency and the Diet, was set forth the facts in a straightforward way; that this should cause any problem seemed strange to me. I had used the name of the Defense Agency for a very simple reason: being very forthright about the facts might, I thought, help persuade my readers that I was on the up-and-up.

In the face of an outright order, however, I could only comply. As instructed, I telephoned the offices of the Asahi Shimbun and asked to speak to the man in charge, a Mr. D. He wasn't in. It was an urgent matter, I said, so I asked them to have D call me back.

"Where can you be reached?" inquired the voice.

"I'm in the office of the director general of the Ministry of Health and Welfare," I said. Whether my reply did the trick or not, I can't say, but in five minutes the phone rang, and D was on the line. I explained the nature of the bureau chief's requests.

"I doubt if alterations are possible at this late date, but I'll talk to the editors and see what can be done," he answered. We waited to see what would happen. In the interim, the officials looked fit to be tied. After a while, D called back.

"Dr. Miyamoto, the printing is finished, and it's gone on to the bookbinders, so nothing can be done. The editors say they'd consider a change if there were some error in what you have written, but that doesn't appear to be the case. I'm sorry to disappoint the director general, but you'll have to tell him we can't go along with his wishes this time."

That was the final reply. As I reported it, the men gathered in the director general's office made sour faces. One of them said to me, "It comes down to doing the right thing and saving face." I wasn't too sure what he meant, but a sympathetic co-worker explained it this way:

"As a result of your article, they might be summoned to testify in the Diet, and the Defense Agency might tell them they don't want any more of their employees on transfer. That's what they're most afraid of."

The Diet and the ministries enjoy a give-and-take relationship, which is apparently why bureaucrats are not supposed to be critical of Diet members. Only the people—the electorate— have the right to criticize the Diet, it seems. Bureaucrats are voters too, if you ask me, but evidently our status as government workers outweighs our status as citizens. Forced to wear two hats—executive and legislative—the Japanese bureaucrat must constantly be on guard during parliamentary questioning to remain noncommittal. Questioners are less interested in engaging in meat-and-potatoes debates over the relative merits of differing plans than they are in undermining the opposition by focusing on minor, nonessential details. These are the sorts of people that bureaucrats must deal with in pushing legislation through. My criticisms of the system were considered likely to provoke them. The real, unspoken complaint was evidently, "Look. Dealing with the Diet is hard enough as it is. Don't do anything to stir those people up."

Making Matters Worse

When the passage about the Diet came under fire, I was called in for yet another meeting with the director general, the personnel director, and, this time, my immediate supervisor.

"What I wrote about the Diet is factual," I began. "Everyone who knows what goes on there agrees that legislative work is actually done by the bureaucracy, and that only people who are incapable of drafting legislation get elected to the Diet in the first place. I wanted to call the entire situation into question."

"It's true that Diet members do rely on bureaucrats to draft legislation," said the director general. "That still doesn't justify the kind of explicitness in your account, does it?"

"If any members of the Diet want to challenge what I have written, let them come directly to me. If any do, I'll tell them that before they criticize me, they ought to learn how to make laws on their own, without any help from the bureaucracy."

"You'll say no such thing," snapped my supervisor. "You really have no common sense."

"None of what passes for common sense around here, you mean. I don't happen to think that the bureaucracy's kind of common sense is always right."

"That's why you go around causing all this trouble," said the personnel director. "You lack sufficient awareness of your duty as a public servant."

"Yeah," added my supervisor, "just who do you think you are? The Diet members have been elected by the people. It's rude to find fault with them."

"Whether or not it's rude is not for you to say but for the Diet members themselves, don't you think? If they want to complain, they should do so directly to me."

"You're awfully cocky," scowled my supervisor.

"It's my policy to speak out plainly about things that strike me as wrong, no matter who may be involved. If that seems like cockiness to you, so be it."

"I don't care what your policy is," he continued. "If you have something to say, wait till you're on the outside. Once you're out of the ministry, you can say or write anything you damn well please."

"Never mind, you two," said the director general. "There's no point in arguing with a zealot. You won't get anywhere. If you want to carry on this discussion, do it somewhere else. All that is beside the point now. The point is, Dr. Miyamoto, we can't have you writing negative criticism of the Diet."

"In any case," I said, "if any of the parliamentarians express dismay at what I have written, please send them directly to me. I will accept full responsibility for dealing with them."

"It's not up to you to accept that responsibility," he answered. "That responsibility lies at the top."

"But sir, you didn't write that article, so why should you take responsibility for it?"

"You belong to the technical advisors group at the Ministry of Health and Welfare. I'm in charge of that group, and if any problem arises out of it, I'm automatically responsible."

"That's strange," I said. "I could understand your taking responsibility if you had interfered in something that one of your subordinates had decided, but why on earth you should take responsibility in a case like this, which happened completely outside your jurisdiction, I can't fathom."

My superiors were thoroughly incensed. All my attempts to justify myself had only made matters worse. What I found most peculiar, though, was that at no time did our discussion focus on the essence of what I had written.

There was no coming together of minds between us. Still, it wasn't the first time this had happened. Since my repatriation, I had stirred up one problem after another at work; but on reflecting back over those experiences, I became aware that whenever I sat down and tried to talk things over with my detractors to get at the source of the problem, we never achieved any sort of accord. Every time this happened, I couldn't help feeling a pang of loneliness.

I may be extremely logical in my approach to things, but I am by no means a stubborn man. I have no interest in saving face or maintaining pride. At least, that's how I seem to myself. And yet, I finally saw that my personality is somehow at the root of the many difficulties I've experienced in the government bureaucracy.

Individuals Are Not Held Accountable

The question of accountability is a good example. In Japan's group-oriented society, as I know very well, the system of accountability outlined by the director general is the general rule. And yet there are aspects of this system which I find hard to swallow. Why should someone have to accept responsibility for everything his subordinates do and say, simply because he happens to be at the head of an organization? Anyone forced into such a position would have to find it oppressive.

If those at the top are held accountable for everything, and those underneath for nothing, then inevitably, things are run by the demerit system. No one wants to incur the boss's wrath. People go out of their way to avoid making mistakes. As a result, the finished product will be remarkably close to perfection. The ability of the Japanese to produce high-quality goods derives in large part from this. There is a downside, however: fear of mistakes leads to a heavy emphasis on precedent, which means continual support for the status quo.

Another characteristic of this system of accountability is that no one takes individual responsibility for anything. Ultimate responsibility lies with the post of the man on top. The individual responsibility of whoever happens to occupy that post is left fuzzy. A system of group evasion of responsibility—or rather, a system of irresponsibility—is set up. Therefore, the one who makes a show of assuming responsibility by giving up his post only receives another post suited to his ability, once the furor has died down. "Taking responsibility" is thus perfunctory, a matter of form and not substance. Among the advanced democratic nations, only Japan has an unclear locus of responsibility, where individuals are never called to account.

I submitted my manuscript for publication at my own discretion, on my own responsibility; at no time did I intend for the director general to take responsibility for what I myself had done. In the bureaucratic world, however, the fact that responsibility rests with the highest-ranking bureaucrat does place effective restraints on individual behavior. Not only is this Japanese system of responsibility intrinsically at odds with the democratic ideal of freedom of speech, it is also a fundamental threat to the idea of liberty.

Sanction for Lies

"Don't go around causing trouble for everybody."

This bit of friendly advice I received from a top administrator is intriguing. Even though those in the highest positions are held accountable for the actions of their subordinates, you never hear anyone say, "Don't cause me any trouble." Instead, they worry about "everybody."

Japanese organizations require their constituent members to identify completely with one another. As a result, one person's opinion becomes what "everybody" thinks, exerting silent coercion on the listener. Any way of thinking judged to have a negative impact on the organization is condemned out of hand in these terms: "Everybody says it's self-centered and self-indulgent." In Japan, to differ from everyone else is perforce to be branded selfish. Yet in the West, those who can speak up for themselves in a rational, logical fashion are esteemed as thoughtful, intelligent people.

The whole notion of *meiwaku*, causing trouble for others, is a bit tricky. It means to do anything that will cause another or others (on the group level or as individuals) to feel dismayed, dissatisfied, displeased, uneasy, or angry. Naturally, there are bound to be individual differences in response; what is *meiwaku* to one person may not be so to another.

The effect of telling someone not to "cause trouble for everyone," however, functions to enforce repression most of the time; stating your own opinion becomes extremely difficult. Any time you express your individuality, you inevitably run the risk of arousing someone's dismay, dissatisfaction, displeasure, unease, or anger. Someone thus ends up suffering *meiwaku*. The only way to avoid "causing trouble for everyone" is to hold yourself to statements sufficiently bland as to provide no emotional stimulus whatever. Even more, you are sometimes compelled to dissemble. When refraining from telling the truth allows people to avoid the hassle of *meiwaku*, a climate is easily engendered in which the truth is unwelcome. This can degenerate into a philosophy that accepts mendacity as the price of not causing trouble.

The Japanese willingness to sanction lies is, I believe, a major source of cultural friction with Western countries that are founded on Christian culture, which teaches people to face the truth unflinchingly in all things. "Even if you have to make trouble for others, you must never tell a lie"; "anyone who cannot face the truth is a moral weakling": this is the Western point of view. Japanese-style "consideration" that sanctions lying is unwarrantable.

The Bureaucrat's Virtues

In the Japanese bureaucratic world, great value is placed on not expressing one's individuality. A certain director general had this to say to me concerning my series of articles:

"A bureaucrat's actions must not be guided by values. If anything, a bureaucrat's only value is *messhi hoko*, sacrificing personal interest to public good. *Sen'yu koraku* [literally, "first distress, later pleasure," or seeking one's own pleasure in life only after the people's happiness is assured] is the goal to which all bureaucrats must aspire. A vice-minister who retires has a happy look on his face. Why? Because now, finally, he can start to enjoy life. You're going about things backwards. If you don't understand the joy of putting off private satisfaction for the sake of your work, you don't deserve to be a government bureaucrat."

This statement is extremely interesting. As an enunciation of the virtues of a bureaucrat, it applies not only to the government bureaucracy but to Japanese society at large, where individuality has no footing.

Soon after I joined the ministry, I was told this by a top official: "A ministry worker (*yakunin*) must be like an actor (*yakusha*); he should be able to handle whatever work he is assigned. There's no place for personal preferences."

Sure enough, *yakunin*, the Japanese word for government bureaucrat, is virtually identical with the word for actor: both begin with the character for "role," followed by different characters meaning "person." In other words, a bureaucrat is someone who skillfully plays a role. But to be able to handle any assigned work/role with equal skill is far from easy. People do, after all, have their likes and dislikes. If people stick to their own policy at work, a real possibility arises of changing direction.

On my first day on the job after being transferred to the

Office of Disease Control, I spread out my things on my new desktop. It so happened that among them were copies of the *International Herald Tribune* and *Time*. My section chief looked at those and said to me with a slightly worried look on his face, "It's interesting the way a desktop changes when someone new occupies the desk. That doesn't matter so much, but I do think it's important that your work show continuity with that of your predecessor."

For a bureaucrat plunged into a world where assigned duties must be carried out without betrayal of preference one way or the other, a strong sense of individuality can only get in the way. That section manager, faced with me as his new assistant, took one look at my belongings and decided I was likely to express my individuality; out of that discovery grew a sense of vague unease as to my suitability for the job.

When you accept that large organizations, as typified by the government bureaucracy, have as a major premise the negation of individuality, a lot of things begin to fall into place. The peace-at-any-price philosophy embodied in the common expression *taika naku*, "without committing any serious errors," (as in "He worked there for thirty long years without committing any serious errors"); the denial of autonomy and creativity; the preference for a perverted equality rather than free competition, harmony rather than policy, and seniority rather than ability: all are founded upon the negation of individuality. The custom of *nemawashi*, consensus-building, helps build an atmosphere of seeming invincibility, as suggested by the ironic popular saying: "Red light—if we all cross together, there's nothing to fear." All of this is inextricably bound with a thoroughgoing denial of the rights of the individual.

Over and over, the ministry officials I spoke to stressed that once I left the ministry, I could do and say as I pleased, but that as long as I was on the "inside," I should hold my tongue. This argument about "insiders" sticking together bears a close connection to the denial of the individual. The conversation below illustrates the logic of "inside vs. outside."

Contents Don't Matter

After the *Monthly Asahi* hit the newsstands, I was called back to the Ministry of Health and Welfare for another meeting. A ministry investigator was brought in this time.

"Just what is this all about?" the investigator demanded.

"I focused on some of the problems concerning vacations, using examples from my own experience," I replied.

"That's not what I'm asking. I want to know your future plans."

"I'm thinking things over. Right now I'm feeling my way."

"I can see no sign whatever that you have any intention of remaining part of the organization," he continued. "Usually people make some effort to do that."

My supervisor then asked, "Aren't you ashamed of yourself for submitting an article like that to the *Asahi*?"

"You would be ashamed of it, so you don't. I wasn't ashamed of it, so I did. Please don't try to force your way of thinking on me."

"Anyway, don't do it again," my supervisor warned.

"Whether I do or not is up to me to decide; it's not up to you to tell me what to do in this matter."

"You live in a different world from us," said the investigator.

"Unfortunately, that appears to be true," I replied.

"Your way of thinking leads to terrible trouble for everyone," said the supervisor.

"The capacity to embrace different ways of thinking is a fundamental part of a democracy."

"Your values are fundamentally different from ours," said the investigator. "I knew you had spent time abroad, so I expected there would be some difference, but I never thought it would be anything like this. You're too different."

"People who don't share our way of thinking will just have to leave," threatened the supervisor.

"Excuse me, but I can't help noticing that no one has questioned me about the contents of the article I wrote."

"I haven't read it and I'm not going to," said the investigator. "The contents don't matter. The issue here is the fact that someone who belongs to the organization would submit a thing like that to a magazine. Someone who shared our values would never have written it in the first place. Your way of thinking has no place in this organization. The only thing for you to do is pack up and get out."

"Most of the people around me at work, anyway, have told me they enjoyed it," I protested.

"How could anybody enjoy a thing like that?" asked the supervisor.

"No," said the investigator, "there are people who say what he wrote was interesting. But there are also people who thought it was offensive. That's the problem. You can't go around writing things that offend people. Especially in bureaucratic circles, problems arise. Your beliefs and ours don't match."

"Maybe they don't at that. I'm happy to do my work as a government official. But I don't want to parrot the dogma with everybody. 'Don't take vacations; help out when somebody moves; when you're sick, use your annual vacation leave; shorten your lunch hour; stay late'—it's all dogma. I'd like to see more attention paid to the abilities of the individual."

"Abilities?" the supervisor said. "You've got a lot of nerve, since you yourself have no abilities to speak of. Leave the government and say anything you want from the outside."

"You seem awfully eager for me to resign, but whether I do or not is an important issue in my life, one that I have to decide for myself. It's not a question of my simply following your instructions."

"Aside from something like bribery," continued the investigator, "we can't fire you—so submit your resignation as soon as
you can. You seem to have your own plans for your life, but in
any case, I don't want to have to see you in this office again."

Foreigners Are Always "Outsiders"

The ministry officials explained to me that the Ministry of
Health and Welfare formed one "village," and that the most
important thing in bureaucratic society was to make a clear distinction between what concerned the village—internal matters—
and what concerned the outside world.

This concept of inside (*uchi*) and outside (*soto*) is uniquely
Japanese. It is symbolized in the Japanese word for foreigner,
gaijin, which means literally "outside person." A clear line is
drawn between inside and outside, and unless they bow to
"inside" dogma in everyday life, those on the "outside" can
never cross over and come in.

No matter how deep their understanding of Japanese culture, or how similar their lifestyle to that of the Japanese
around them, foreigners are always "outside." No other industrialized nation is nearly so exclusive as Japan.

In recent years, Japan has been criticized by other nations
for having closed markets—another phenomenon that resolves
into a question of the exclusivity of the village mentality.

A friend of mine who works for a news service had this to
say: "What you say is right. But if there were someone like you
in my company, I wouldn't like it, either. I'd probably do just
what they're doing at the Ministry of Health and Welfare,
which is plot how to get rid of you. That's why the Asahi Shimbun Publishing Company can afford to print what you write in
the first place—it doesn't concern them. If one of their own staff
tried to do the same thing, they'd never offer him space in a
million years."

In Japanese society, for an insider to criticize his own inner circle is taboo. I had broken that taboo, as became very clear to me after my article appeared in the *Monthly Asahi*.

At first, the organization had forcibly urged me to restrain what I said and wrote and to adopt the same behavior as everyone else, under penalty of ostracism. When the taboo was finally broken, I began to be ostracized in fact.

I learned something else from the experience: that "village" harmony and peace are preserved at the cost of the personal life of the individual. But can such peace be said to be founded on real pacifism?

Those who so jealously guard the peace of the "village" scarcely care what happens outside the village borders. Recreation areas littered with trash, drivers who casually toss litter out the window while driving down the street, and even the well-known proverb, *tabi no haji wa kakisute* ("On a journey, cast off shame")—all arise from this mentality. There are many other instances: During a recession, foreign workers, including foreign-born workers of Japanese parentage, are quickly let go; Japanese workers are rarely if ever fired.

What happens when this mentality impinges on dealings with foreign countries? Since the harmony of life inside Japan is of preeminent importance, people are all too likely to feel that the effects of Japanese competition on foreign countries—the "outside"—are none of their affair. The Japanese economy, being based on the sacrifice of the private life of the individual, flexes its "economic animal" muscles and seeks to enlarge itself by similarly sacrificing the personal lives of foreigners. Under those circumstances, how could Japan escape criticism from overseas?

My bombshell article in the *Monthly Asahi* brought me the opprobrium of my bosses and a great deal of notoriety, but it had the opposite effect on some people. Many of my co-workers in the ministry came up to me privately and said they were glad that I had been so outspoken, that everyone thought the way I did but no one could say so, because they were part of the organization.

The head of a hospital affiliated with a national university, one with close ties to the Ministry of Health and Welfare, took the trouble of writing me a letter of warm encouragement. I received extremely favorable reactions from other acquaintances, too. "I enjoyed reading it," said one. "Is there going to be a sequel?" Someone else commented, "The bureaucratic world is really old-fashioned, isn't it? You need to let in some fresh air."

These reactions were very encouraging to me. I must also express my thanks to the many readers who expressed concern over my future, wondering, "Is it all right for you to go so far?"

The nail that sticks out gets hammered down, they say. But there's no point in giving up now. If a nail sticks out far enough, it can't be hammered down. I mean to muster up my courage and become that nail.

chapter 6

The Masochistic Personality and The Psychology of Bullying

Keep Away from Miyamoto

After a few of my articles had appeared in the *Monthly Asahi*, I received a phone call one afternoon from a friend. "Listen," he told me, "someone just asked me, 'What do you hang around with Miyamoto for?' I said it was because I admired you, but it looks like there's going to be pressure on us to keep our distance. Thought you ought to know."

At lunch, another friend told me of similar moves in our own ministry. "It doesn't bother me, but some of the guys are saying the pressure will make it harder for them to go on being your friend."

And a top official gave me this warning: "Bureaucrats are easily intimidated. They worry most of all about protecting their own hide, so as long as you stay on here, you'll find you don't have many friends. Of course, a lot of people do support you internally and admire your honesty, which is all the more reason why you should leave here as soon as you can and make new friends somewhere else. I'm saying this for your own good."

I couldn't help thinking he sounded just like the Japanese schoolyard bully who picks on weaker classmates, ordering the rest of the class not to play with So-and-so any more. Planting the suggestion that people should have nothing to do with me was nothing less than a form of bullying. Adult society is not immune to the phenomenon.

Some sort of reaction to my articles was inevitable, of course, but I'd never expected anything like this. My writings contained no personal attacks. All I had done was point out some problems in the present bureaucratic organization based on my own experience, out of a firm conviction that in order for Japan to assume a position of leadership among developed nations, things would have to change. Yet my basic premise was ignored; the attention focused solely on my disruption of office harmony. The response was illogical and emotional, and it culminated in corporate bullying.

The Mini-Dictator

This was not my first encounter with such bullying. I was plagued with it when I first joined the Health and Welfare Ministry in 1986. Eleven years before that, I had gone to the United States and plunged into a completely new environment, where I was never once made the object of bullying, neither during the first year nor at any time thereafter.

It came as a considerable shock to me, therefore, that I

should be exposed to such treatment in my own country, where I had returned eager to make a contribution in my field. The harassment I was subjected to quickly turned me into an insomniac. Let me give a few examples.

With overtime work taken for granted in the ministries, it is customary for the director of general affairs to pay for employees' dinners out of the slender resources available to him in the budget. One day, we were served *domburimono*—large bowls of steaming rice with a topping of meat and/or vegetables. Since the dish tastes best when eaten hot, I took a break from work and started to dig in. Some others did the same. One bossy official, however, singled me out for reprimand:

"Miyamoto, you still have work to do, don't you? How can you eat? You'd better wait till you've come to a stopping place. You're new around here, and you barely understand what to do in the first place—what business have you got thinking you can eat dinner with the rest of us, anyway!" Still unused to Japan, I went back to my work in meek surprise.

In the Japanese bureaucracy, certain people always have the authority to run their division like a mini-dictator. They may be relatively low in rank, but generally they have extensive practical experience and know far more of the ins and outs of the ministry than a young deputy director could possibly hope to know. Since seniority is all-important in the bureaucratic world, power is commensurate with the number of years spent on the job, not necessarily with position. Such people's influence therefore often exceeds that of the director. It's not hard to see why they want to throw their weight around, since they are after all eminently qualified to do so.

It is also true, however, as I found out, that such men can be truculent, contemptuous, and abusive to deputies new on the job. Apparently, returnees from overseas like me arouse their envy. They are relentless in their attack.

One day, the same bossy guy said to me, "God, are you lucky.

135

Here you are a deputy director, after just joining the Ministry of Health and Welfare. You get more pay than the rest of us, too. Just don't get on your high horse about being some kind of mental health expert now, will you?"

Afterwards, I realized I responded to this remark in the wrong way. My mistake lay in protesting, "Hey, the salary I earned in the United States was easily ten times what I make now. I have to pinch pennies, believe me." This statement riled him to no end. After that, whenever ministry people got together, he made a point of sneering at me with open envy:

"Deputy Director Miyamoto here led a very luxurious life in America. Look at how he's dressed. He's got wonderful taste, doesn't he? Of course, you and I haven't got the money to approach his level. It must be nice to be rich."

Never Ask About What You Don't Know

In any new environment, there are always lots of unknowns. One day, I was told to take some papers over to the Ministry of Home Affairs. Before starting work in Japan, I had taught at several universities in the States, and I considered myself something of an authority on mental health care; my expertise was the very reason I had been hired, and yet it seemed to tick some people off. Day after day, I was used as a courier or ordered to make copies—a far cry from what I'd thought my new job would entail. It wasn't hard for me to see why people would be jealous; I had landed a responsible post in the ministry without working my way up from below. But that didn't make it any easier to take.

I decided to grin and bear it. Still, I'd been away from Japan for eleven years. I knew the Ministry of Home Affairs was somewhere nearby, but, not knowing the exact location, asked a colleague, "Uh, where's the Ministry of Home Affairs again?"

"Miyamoto's been away from Japan so long, he doesn't

know anything. What a pain!" the despot instantly cried out, in full earshot of the neighboring department. The others all burst out laughing.

Perhaps fearing reprisals from that vindictive man, no one would tell me where to go. I was angered by their spinelessness and decided I'd find it myself. I picked up the telephone and dialed information. No sooner had I done so than my tormenter complained again:

"What the hell do you need a telephone number for?"

"I'm going to call the place and find out where it is."

"Don't use the telephone for something like that," he said curtly.

The director, having returned to the department in the interim, could stand it no longer and beckoned me over to his desk. Before giving me the directions I needed, he offered this encouragement: "You'll catch on, don't worry. That's the kind of place it is around here. After a while, they'll leave you alone." To this day I am grateful for his kindness.

Just after I joined the ministry, a meeting was held during which the word *nichi-i* was tossed around. I could tell it was an abbreviated form of some organization's name, but I didn't really understand. It was a key word at the meeting, however, and unless I knew what it meant, I couldn't follow the discussion.

On the principle that when you don't understand something, you should speak up and ask for an explanation, I inquired, "What does *nichi-i* mean?" To my surprise, everyone gave me a cold stare, as if to say, "Don't ask dumb questions. You just hold up the progress of the meeting." Not until after the meeting was over did someone tell me that *nichi-i* was short for *Nihon Ishikai,* or the Japan Medical Association. I had been put in my place, and the experience was intimidating. After that, if a word came up that I didn't know, I never asked publicly what it meant.

The difference from the way I'd been treated during my eleven years in America was striking. There, people kindly fill you in on anything you don't happen to know. Coming back to Japan, I was taken aback when people said things like, "Everybody knows this, so you should, too," or, "It's your fault for not knowing." Thinking about it, I realized that for me to be ignorant was only natural, and to be made fun of on that account made no sense at all. From then on I changed my attitude, becoming more defiant. "I have a perfect right not to know this, and if you expect me to, you're the ones who are crazy." That, as it turned out, was the best way to escape their browbeating and bullying.

Don't Be Different

In the ministries every morning, the female secretaries make tea for everyone. When I arrived a little late one morning, the secretary in my division was bringing me tea as usual, when the same autocrat said in a deliberately loud voice, "Don't bring Miyamoto any tea."

My jaw dropped. Naturally, there is no law that says if you're late to work you get no tea. I had never heard of anyone being told such a thing.

As I observed more closely, however, I discovered that I was not alone. One other man—also a newcomer—was getting the same "no-tea" treatment. Not only was he new like myself, but he looked different from the others. His clothes were more stylish, his neckties more elegant and worn with more panache. Unlike me, he did make some effort to blend in with everyone, but because he lacked a certain crudeness, he ended up standing out anyway. His conversation, too, was pleasantly witty, and clearly he was a man of high cultural attainment. He also had the ability to work at his own pace and get his work done smoothly and efficiently.

However, anyone with so much charm, and so unlike his peers, is a prime candidate for bullying—whether or not he has just returned from abroad. There is an unwritten law in the bureaucracy that basically says, "Thou shalt not be different from thy co-workers."

Masochists

As I observed this other man being picked on by the others, I realized that bullying in Japan has another aspect. The other man's view of life—like my own, I might add—had an element of playfulness. He believed in injecting a modicum of that spirit into all areas of life and enjoying himself. The person who can have fun without worrying about what others think is a far cry from the masochistic type who exists solely to render service to Japan, Inc. Those who are up to their ears in Japanese-style collectivism evidently find such independent, fun-loving personalities extremely hard to deal with. Anyone lacking in sufficient masochistic tendencies is bullied by the group, which wants to see one and all acquire the same degree of masochism. The act of bullying also serves as a way to test the extent of the newcomer's latent masochistic tendencies.

If even one member of the group believed that bullying was wrong, at some point that person would seek some way to stop it. But while some may sympathize secretly with the victim, no one acts to put a stop to this pernicious practice, and no one speaks out in protest. This can only mean that somewhere inside, they all support the act of bullying. Taking the punishment is the only way the newcomer can become a full member of the group. Applying the whip to yourself and demonstrating to the group your ability to endure the pain is the way to earn recognition as a full-fledged purveyor of Japan, Inc.

Each year, when the spring and summer high school baseball tournaments get underway, bureaucrats are glued to their

TV sets, work forgotten. The attraction? The high school kids go to desperate lengths to be able to play in Koshien Stadium, the tournament site near Kobe, and push themselves to the furthest limits of masochistic behavior in pursuit of their dream. That spirit no doubt touches something deep in the bureaucrat's soul. And that's why it is so important in the bureaucracy for the group to find out how much tolerance for masochism newcomers may possess.

Not long after I joined the ministry, I participated in drafting a legal revision. After staying up night after night, by the final day for submission of the bill, everyone was short on sleep, catching catnaps when they could. Just before dawn, the work entered the final stage of preparing copies and binding them together. Exhausted, I took advantage of the lull to grab an hour's sleep. When I returned, however, the project supervisor gave me a sound scolding: "How dare you go off and sleep when we're this busy? Of all the selfish behavior!"

"Everyone's been taking naps when they could, all along," I protested. "Why single me out for complaint?" I was still unsure of how to deal with such attacks in those days, however, and, though I hate to admit it, I added an apology: "I'm very sorry."

Any admission of weakness on the part of the victim only emboldens those harassing him. Wanting to look over the result of all our labors, I requested a copy, only to hear him bellow, "You've got so much time on your hands, find it yourself!" He was a big, hulking man, with a voice to match. I had no choice but to rub my sleepy eyes and put together a set of the voluminous materials as best I could.

Experiences such as this taught me that newcomers earn recognition as full-fledged members of Japan Inc. based not on their abilities but on the extent to which they become others' hands and feet, demonstrating their willingness to drive themselves physically. In other words, they must show off the limits of masochism of which they are capable. If those limits are the same as, or greater than, everyone else's, the lucky newcomer receives his stamp of approval.

The moment the group senses that the pain of self-flagellation has changed to pleasure, bullying ceases. Therefore, the first thing to do when you enter the bureaucracy is not to demonstrate how capable you are at your job but to let everyone know what a glutton for punishment you are. When the truth of this first hit me, I couldn't get over the bizarreness of bureaucratic values. At the same time, I vowed to myself that anytime those values were forced on me, even by a superior, I would put my foot down firmly.

Enjoying Others' Struggles

To this day, I have never broken that vow. Here is an example. When I was sent to the Defense Agency, I was told by the deputy director of general affairs to run out and buy a boxed lunch.

"Are you sure you haven't got the wrong person?" I replied politely. "I'm here as a specialist. I'm not going out to buy anyone a boxed lunch."

He tried to justify himself. "You've only been around for a year or so, isn't that right, Miyamoto? You need to experience things from the bottom up."

"I didn't come here to be anyone's lackey. You and I have fundamentally different ways of thinking. You're saying that even the driver of a bullet train should be out punching tickets. I happen to disagree."

Whether what I said made any impression on him I don't know, but he never again asked me to do odd jobs.

Bullying is an insidious phenomenon that can take many forms. As another example, when we were compiling answers for parliamentary interpellation, I was forced to rewrite my contributions countless times for trivial reasons. Watching me struggle, they would nudge one another and say things like,

"Miyamoto's Japanese is rusty. This is just what he needs."
I have no doubt whatsoever that they were enjoying themselves
at my expense. Often, the wording that won final approval dif-
fered hardly at all from the first version which I wrote without
laboring over.

Superior English Is Not Acceptable

I once spoke with mothers of children who had returned to
Japan after a period abroad. I told them that people in Japan
sometimes gave me a hard time about my English, complaining
that my accent was so good that they couldn't understand a
word I said.

One of the mothers replied, "Dr. Miyamoto, don't you
know? Children who've come back from overseas have to try as
hard as they can to speak English poorly at school."

"That's only common sense," agreed another.

"Yes, if they speak too well, the other children pick on them,"
chimed in a third. I was further taken aback to hear that the
children's teachers often took the lead in such bullying.

The trials of returnee children are a relatively recent phenomenon. What happens to children who study overseas and
then return to Japan? They are criticized for things like stating
their opinions too clearly, questioning what the teacher says,
chattering during lunchtime instead of eating in silence, and
lacking in a spirit of cooperation. They are urged to go along
with the group, and those who do not are made targets of bullying. That in a nutshell is exactly what happened to me in the
bureaucracy.

In Japan, bullying is essentially a tool for forcing the individual to accept the logic of the group. In schools, as I said
before, the teacher often takes the lead, though such bullying
is by no means confined to school settings—my own case
being a good example of what goes on in adult society. It is sad,

however, that schoolchildren fluent in English and other languages should feel compelled to hide their abilities, in line with the proverb that "a wise hawk hides his talons." That this practice has become "common sense" for returnees shows how truly parochial Japanese society is. In this age of increased focus on education and deepening international ties, any nation that is unable to draw out the individual abilities of its children doesn't stand a chance of excelling in global competition.

The type of group bullying typified in the treatment accorded returnee schoolchildren is unique to Japan. When a Japanese goes overseas, enters an alien culture, and then returns with an un-Japanese-like aura about him or her, the group resorts to bullying tactics in order to purge the individual of alien influence.

In a gesture of friendliness, I once accompanied a few of my co-workers to a karaoke bar. Someone yelled, "Miyamoto, you're fresh from America, sing us a song in English!" Now, I must confess that I am completely tone-deaf. Even so, they urged me to perform. The more I resisted, the more determined they became.

"You must know one song. It doesn't matter how well you sing it, so come on. We insist."

A fat book was handed to me. Someone explained, "This contains a list of songs. There's got to be something you know."

"Yeah, let's hear you sing with that un-Japanese pronunciation of yours!" added someone else, while from across the room a voice cried out, "The show won't go on until Miyamoto sings!"

My attention was carefully drawn to the little heart next to some song titles, which I was told meant the lyrics were good and risqué. If that's what they were after, they could damn well get up and sing their songs themselves, I thought, but group pressure is hard to resist. They came at me so insistently that finally I gave in, chose something, and got up on the stage.

"Let's hear it, America!" Jibes flew. When other people sang, no one had paid any attention, and there'd been only scattered, polite applause; yet now I found all eyes on me. While I was musing about that, words began to appear on the Tele-prompter. Hastily, I started to sing, but I couldn't keep up. My voice was too high, and I knew that all in all, I was making a spectacle of myself. Midway through, the director took pity on me and sang along, so I got through it somehow, but as far as I was concerned, I might as well have been in a basement of KGB headquarters in Moscow: it was sheer torture.

Dress Like Everybody Else

Bullying even extends to matters of taste in dress. I am quite interested in the fashion world; while I was in the United States, I once worked part-time as a stylist and fashion consultant. Naturally, I am fussy about what I wear. This seems to make me an eyesore at the bureaucracy, where people rub it in by asking me sarcastic questions about the width of my pants, the pattern and price of my suits, my designer's name, the maker of my neckties, and even the style of underwear I have on. Apparently the message is, "Look like the rest of us. Italian fashions are hardly appropriate for a bureaucrat."

One day, I received this advice: "Instead of wasting time try-ing to make stupid statements about yourself, why not try to blend with everybody else?" His choice of words fascinated me. Whether I was indeed wasting time on something stupid was a matter of opinion; but in this social climate, if the group decides something is stupid, one and all are required to think so. As I observed the collectivist ways of ministry officials, I sometimes wondered what difference there was, if any, between this society and that of prewar, militaristic Japan.

In any case, the advice about my clothes and the karaoke episode were typical examples of harassment.

An Eye for an Eye

The longer I stayed at the bureaucracy, the more adept I became at dealing with bullying. My approach in compiling answers to parliamentary interpellation, a process that takes till dawn, provides a good example of my tactical change.

Since the work lasted all night anyway, I always began writing my answers toward midnight, when everybody was sleepy and less inclined to torment me. While the malicious supervisor waited on the lookout for me, ready to give me a piece of his mind, I typically went to a nearby French restaurant and sipped wine. Around ten thirty, I would return to the office and set to work. The supervisor, seeing me at work with my face flushed from the wine, would speak to me sharply. Here follows a typical conversation:

"Where have you been? You can't just walk out the door when there's important work to be done here!"

"I was having an important discussion with one of my bosses."

"About work?"

"No, about the connection between alcohol and circulatory disorders."

"Who is he? Who would sit around with you and talk about a thing like that, at a time like this?"

"No one you know. And it's really none of your business."

"If your discussion was so damn important, why are you red in the face? If you've been drinking beer, that was awfully imprudent."

"Not beer, wine. Research shows that red wine lowers cholesterol in the blood. I thought it was important to act on those findings. Besides, discussions of wine extend into discussions of culture in general. And besides, if I'm imprudent, then so are the director general and the minister himself. They're all drinking, too."

"It's our job to write answers for the parliamentary questioning. You can't do your job if you're drunk."

"You had a beer around six o'clock, didn't you, sir? How are the answers coming along, anyway? Are they done?"

"Miyamoto, that's your job! You were supposed to come up with draft answers!"

"Was I? I'd completely forgotten. If I get right to work now, I'll be finished after midnight. You seem to like sleeping on the sofa in the director general's office better than your own bed, so why not go in there now and catch a few winks?"

"I only sleep on that sofa when I'm too busy to go home. I'm not like you, Miyamoto, always goofing off. It's unbelievable to me that you could have forgotten about this assignment! That's dereliction of duty. Besides, it's my responsibility to go over what you write."

"No, your using the director general's office like a hotel is the manifestation of a subconscious desire to be director general."

"I don't recall asking you for a psychoanalysis."

I finally finished up a little after eleven o'clock, by which time the project supervisor had gone to sleep. With a side glance at him, I handed my written reply directly to the deputy secretary of the general affairs department—thus neatly bypassing the supervisor from my own division.

Such treatment meant a severe loss of face for him. I knew this full well, but since he was always coming down on me, I did it anyway, hoping that it might take him down a peg or two. Sure enough, when he woke up he was furious, but there was nothing he could do about it.

Japanese-style bullying uses the threat of ostracism to attack people's deep psychology and arouse anxiety. "You'll find yourself all alone," your tormenters will say, or "If you leave here, you won't be able to support yourself anywhere." Psychological pressure is brought to bear in a multitude of ways. Such bullying is extremely sly and deals its victim a heavy blow. The younger the victim, the larger the scar. Those who engage in bullying have much to answer for.

Bullying is a form of persecution. Unfortunately, this dishonorable act is more or less symbolic of Japanese culture. In my case, the bullying continued persistently for about my first year on the job. The following year, however, when I was transferred to the Defense Agency, it disappeared. A friend explained it this way: "People on loan from other ministries are 'guests.' That's why they're let alone. Which is all the more reason for you to give them no cause to talk about you behind your back."

Guests from outside are spared bullying. Everyone is smiling and affable to them, but never are they admitted inside. Bullying, like hazing, is a rite of passage that earns its victims admission to the inner circle. That this antiquated ritual holds sway among members of the government bureaucracy, who are closest to the international community, gives some indication of the primitive level of Japan's internationalization.

Not Everybody Approves

I don't want to leave the impression that all bureaucrats enjoy bullying. I have met any number of kind and sympathetic people, including the director of my division. Lots of other people have also passed through the ordeal of bullying and, knowing the mental and physical pressure it brings to bear on the victim, willingly offer what help they can.

One day not long after I'd arrived, a colleague came up and called me out into the corridor as I was receiving the usual onslaught from all sides.

"I was the victim before you came along," he told me. "They're not bad at heart. Just give them some time." Besides comforting me verbally in this way, he showed other kindnesses as well, such as arranging for me to leave early sometimes instead of staying till all hours with the rest.

I once needed to locate some old documents, but I had no idea where to look. The section chief who wanted them knew where they were but wouldn't tell me. Even so, he complained that my work was overdue. Another deputy director, several years my senior, looked on at one of our exchanges and then took me aside. "The guy means no harm," he said. "Don't hold it against him." Then he handed me the file I needed.

Another time, as I was heading home on the train with a colleague, he clutched the train strap and reflected, "You have a hard time of it, don't you. Coming to a strange new place, only to be met with an onslaught of bullying. If there's ever anything you don't understand, just ask me, and I'll fill you in." It is impossible to describe the overwhelming gratitude that fills you when someone offers help when you need it most. Without the kindness of such people, I'm sure that even someone as thick-skinned as myself would have given up.

Abnormal Psychology

Bullying is a general phenomenon. It is practiced against those who are emotionally weak, those with a physical weakness or handicap, and those who are envied by others for any reason. It is especially common among young people aged fifteen or sixteen. But through my experiences at the Ministry of Health and Welfare, I realized that Japan has its own distinctive brand of bullying, one not found in other countries. In Japan, bullying is condoned by group society, even among adults. This is a major difference from the situation in Western countries.

In the United States, where I spent many years, among people past puberty you hardly ever encounter acts of bullying done in public view. Group bullying of an individual is all but unheard of. Bullying is considered part of a child's psychological makeup, gradually receding into the subconscious as the child matures.

In the West, a bully is thought of as someone who enjoys watching others suffer, and bullying is diagnosed as an abnormal state of mind. Accordingly, adults who think nothing of engaging in bullying are looked on with contempt as cases of arrested development or people with immature personalities. At times, their own mental stability may be questioned. The mind-set that takes pleasure in the pain of others belongs in the world of sado-masochism. Thus in a real sense, anyone who engages in bullying is plunging himself or herself into a world of sexual perversion and abnormal psychology.

The desire to bully or torment exists to a degree in every human heart. Most of the time, however, it is tucked away, unactualized. Certain abnormal circumstances—war, riots, disasters—can cause normal restraints to fall away, so that the latent desire to bully develops into sheer, cold-blooded murderousness. Nazi persecution of the Jews is a good example. The only way such full-scale persecution could have gone on was for ordinary people to support it en masse, either consciously or unconsciously.

We cannot put an end to bullying. Yet it is certainly possible to apply restraints that will suppress that mentality and keep it from emerging. Once one member of a group begins bullying, however, inhibitions may fail, bringing the urge to the fore. As long as people expect the group to act as an inhibitor on their impulses, bullying can emerge with impunity, the way it did in my experience at the Ministry of Health and Welfare.

Treated Like a Criminal

After returning to Japan, I heard of a shocking incident involving a "mock funeral." At a certain elementary school, one little boy was made the frequent target of bullying. One day, the class decided to try a new prank: they would all act as if their classmate had actually died. A large square card was passed around for people to write condolences on, which they all did. The mock funeral engendered intense media attention for two reasons: first, because the victim committed suicide shortly thereafter, and second, because the boy's homeroom teacher had a hand in the "funeral" arrangements.

This sort of abuse demonstrates the terrible cruelty of which humans are capable. The teacher's participation is beyond belief. Had such an incident occurred in the United States, the teacher would not only have had his teaching credentials revoked, but would undoubtedly have been prosecuted as a criminal and sent to jail or treated as a mental aberrant and incarcerated in a mental institution. When I heard of this incident, I was embarrassed for my fellow Japanese and wondered how on earth such a thing could have happened.

How to Deal with Bullying

During my experience of bullying at the Ministry of Health and Welfare, I learned something interesting: neither the leader of the bullying nor those who silently went along with him had their own outlook; their individuation was incomplete. Furthermore, they all shared a relative inability to develop thoughts in a logical fashion and a tendency to be swept by emotion.

These discoveries gave me a way to counterattack. My tactic was to engage the ringleader in discussion and argue him down. Under logical attack, lack of individuation leads quickly to disintegration of the self.

When I employed this tactic, the bullying ceased, and I was able to construct my own world, safe from trespassers. I will say, however, that those who choose to respond to bullying in this way must be prepared to endure isolation.

Being the target of bullying taught me something else: once

the group perceives that their efforts have no effect on you, they will leave you alone. Lasting that long, however, is no easy task. Here, for the sake of returnees of all ages, I will sum up the know-how I have acquired for repelling would-be bullies.

- Don't reveal your weaknesses to the group.
- Assume a defiant attitude.
- Emphasize your abilities.
- Attack your opponent's weak points.
- Embarrass your opponent.
- Let your opponent know how strong you are.

Bullying is a form of discrimination. The first step in true internationalization is to nurture the kind of tolerance that allows you to share the values of someone in your own organization, even if they may be different from your own. The mentality that seeks to get rid of those who are different by bullying them and thus preserve the harmony of the group can only foster discrimination. When stories about bullying no longer fill the pages of our newspapers, then and only then can we say that Japanese society has become truly international.

CHAPTER 7

The Three Great Principles of Life in the Japanese Bureaucracy

The Company Song and the National Anthem

Not long ago I was invited to attend an informal meeting of the Tokyo division of the American Chamber of Commerce in Japan, where I had an opportunity to have an extended conversation with a Mr. A., an American working for a Japanese company. After two years in Japan, he was perplexed by many aspects of Japanese society. I tried to demystify things for him.

(Readers may notice a change in my tone in this chapter as I take a more supportive Japanese position in this reconstructed conversation with an American working for a Japanese company. In response to the problems and criticisms he raises, I

153

chose to take a devil's advocate position and respond as a typical Japanese might, a decision that served to highlight some of the differences under discussion.)

"Japan is impossible for me to figure out," he said. "The first thing every morning at work, we all recite in unison something called the 'company precepts.' What on earth is that all about? It seems to me like a total waste of time."

"It's a kind of ceremony in which people pledge their solidarity to the corporate village, promising one another to do their best. At some companies, everyone sings the company song as well," I replied.

"Really? Why do they do that?"

"Well, even in the States, you like to sing the national anthem to reinforce a sense of national unity, don't you?"

"Only at national events. I've never heard of any school or company where people sang the school song, or the company song, every day."

"Think of it this way. In Japan, every organization is a kind of mini-nation. So the company song corresponds to the national anthem, sung as a demonstration of allegiance. Lots of people think that spirit of allegiance is the key to Japan's productivity," I offered.

"I can't really agree with that," said A. "My co-workers hardly do much to enhance productivity."

"How do you mean?"

"Well, I recite the company precepts along with everybody else, figuring it's good for my Japanese. As soon as that's over, I get right to work. Almost everybody else starts reading the newspaper or drinking a leisurely cup of tea. They certainly don't look like they take their work very seriously," he said.

"Japanese productivity isn't the result of hard work that you can point a finger at; it's based much more on a widespread notion of sacrificing individual life."

"By the same token, couldn't you say that Japanese productivity doesn't rise unless employees all get together to recite the company precepts or sing the company song?" A asked. It certainly was an interesting way to look at it. "The company is a place to earn your daily bread," he continued. "At least, that's what it is to me. But listening to you, it sounds as if in Japan the company comes first, and the individual takes low priority."

"Well, yes. In Japan the company does come first, and employees exist solely for the purpose of making the company stronger. The organization does not exist for the purpose of enriching individual lives."

"In that case, why would anybody want to go on working?"

"That's where the company precepts and company song come in. They instill in the workers a spirit of unity that enables them to work together as a harmonious whole. Japanese have a strong sense of dedication."

"Or you could say it's a sophisticated kind of brainwashing," he added.

"Hmm, I guess that's one way of looking at it. My own opinion is that Japanese seek an emotional stronghold in their company."

"Well, all I know is, the Japanese psyche is constructed very conveniently for the people running companies," he pronounced.

"That may be, but I can assure you the company managers aren't really bent on exploiting people's psychic weaknesses."

"Maybe so, but it seems to me that in Japan, devotion to your work is no guarantee of a better life."

"That's a serious problem, one that Japan has got to deal with. Still, lots of people are satisfied with the status quo. After all, once you're a member of the organization, provisions are made for your wedding, for your children's schooling and job-hunting, and for funerals. You're looked after all the way. That's why I say there's give and take, a mutual support system."

"I still say that at my company, there's too much wasted time."

"But you see, that wasted time is exactly what makes Japanese companies function so well."

"Isn't that's a little contradictory?"

"From a logical standpoint, yes. But the sense of unity that emerges from all that waste is what lies behind the high productivity of Japanese companies. Which is why, ultimately, Western-style management is unnecessary and nonexistent in Japan."

The Code and Self-Sacrifice

Mr. A continued, "There are examples of Western-style leadership here, though. Look at Sony's Akio Morita, or Shuichiro Honda of Honda Motors."

"They're the exceptions," I said. "The majority of Japanese CEOs don't worry about how to bring out the individuality or innate abilities of their employees in order to raise production; they worry about how to maintain harmony among the employees. They see that as the way to achieve higher productivity. And that, you see, leads straight to the idea of total identification between the corporation and the individual."

"It could also mean in effect that the individual is never allowed to stand on his own," he answered.

"That's right. Unlike most Westerners, most Japanese don't live their lives according to any definite set of principles, so there's a tendency for people to scatter off in their own directions. To prevent that, some sort of centripetal force is necessary. Again, that's where the company precepts and the company song come in."

"Sorry? I don't quite follow you."

"Think of it this way. By reciting the company precepts and singing the company song, people are promising one another that they'll abide by the village rules."

"Yeah, but what's that got to do with higher productivity? Aren't you stretching things a little?"

"Village society is extremely closed off. The most important part of the village code is that everyone should always stay together. And the code makes no allowances for individual freedom. Submissive obedience is all. That setup is effective in raising productivity and constitutes what I think can be called a system of self-sacrifice for the benefit of the group."

"I see," he said. "You're saying self-sacrifice is what makes it okay for people to linger over a cup of coffee or read the newspaper."

"Yes, and nowhere is the spirit of self-sacrifice more in evidence than in government offices. That's why you have the three great principles of life in government offices: don't be late, don't take time off, and don't do any work. When I first entered public service, a director general kindly told me that anyone who followed those rules could make section chief at the very least, even if his work wasn't up to par."

The Three Great Principles

"'Don't be late,'" I continued, "means that you must be at work—that is, at your desk—before anyone else; you don't actually have to be working. You could be reading the paper, or looking at a comic book, or having a cup of coffee. The important thing is to let people around you know that you arrived before starting time.

"The second principle, 'Don't take time off,' means, as far as possible, you avoid taking paid vacations. Even if you get sick, you don't take time off until you've let your co-workers see you suffering with a fever. And when you do take off because of sickness, then and only then do you use your paid leave. Officially guaranteed sick leave goes unused. It's also important not only to work overtime but to perform a kind of unpaid "voluntary" overtime. This overtime exists in a multitude of forms: sympathy overtime, which means staying late with co-workers when they have extra work to do, even if you don't; study groups and research teams; take-home work; going out for a few drinks with your superiors; Sunday golf, section trips, baseball tournaments, sports days; helping someone move; attending weddings and funerals...the list goes on and on. The idea is to demonstrate your willingness to sacrifice your own time in order to contribute to the organization."

"I've gone out drinking without giving it too much thought, and I've participated in company sports events too. I never realized there was such deep meaning involved," A said.

"I used to be assigned to the Office of Disease Control. That office deals with virtually every form of human disease, so there were a large number of research teams with direct assignments from the Ministry of Health and Welfare. I was taken aback by the inordinate number of study meetings and research conferences held, almost always on Saturdays. My first official business after being assigned there was to send out a notice to the heads of all the research teams."

"Saying what?"

"Saying that from then on, study meetings and research conferences were no longer to be held on weekends and holidays. They had to be scheduled on weekdays, between the hours of nine and five. Since the research all had the backing of the Ministry of Health and Welfare, I was responsible for showing up each time in order to say a few words and hear the teams' results. With upwards of sixty teams in all, I would have had to spend every weekend of the year attending meetings. At the time I was already putting in a lot of voluntary overtime, so I had not the slightest inclination to give up any more of my free time."

"Where I work," said A, "they're very strict about official statements like that. I'm impressed that the Japanese bureaucracy would allow you to send out such a drastic announcement."

"That's because during times of personnel change, there's tremendous upheaval in government offices, and the controls become surprisingly lax. I took advantage of the general confusion."

"Still, your supervisor must have looked it over."

"No, I did it all on my own authority, without seeking his approval. Chaos gives you surprising freedom of action."

"So what was the result?"

"All hell broke loose."

"I haven't been in Japan all that long yet, but somehow that's not hard to imagine."

"If you can imagine that much, you know a lot about Japanese society. Anyway, there was a division of opinion. One professor criticized me up and down for lacking in all common sense and having no grasp of reality."

"Did your supervisor get in trouble as well?" he asked.

"He apparently got a fair number of complaints over the telephone. He was quite broad-minded, though, so he never complained about my issuing the statement without his approval. What surprised me even more, he actually supported my stand."

"I work for a trading company, so we have a lot of contact with government officials. My overwhelming impression is that they're awfully inflexible. It's nice to know there's an exception."

"Yes," I said, "but he's not with the Ministry of Health and Welfare anymore. People who can clearly distinguish between desirable and undesirable, and take action accordingly, don't get far in the ministries."

"Interesting. It's just the opposite from the States, then. I see what you mean, though, about the importance here of not taking any time off. What about the other principle you mentioned, 'Do no work'? Doesn't that contradict the one about taking no time off?" he asked.

"No, because it's more complicated than it sounds. It means that you must look as if you are working, without actually getting anything done. Specifically, it means you are to avoid undertaking any fresh business as an employee in the executive branch of the government."

"Why is that?"

"Suppose, for example, you know that a certain policy will definitely benefit the people. If you try to implement it on your own, you're bound to stir up opposition. If you push it through anyway and it should happen to fail, you will of course be called to account. The Japanese bureaucracy operates on the demerit system; people seldom receive credit on their work record for any positive changes they may have brought about. Therefore, the smart thing to do is to lie low and try not to accumulate any black marks against your name. This is the quintessential bureaucrat. Once you have a black mark, your career is in jeopardy. Besides, if you act on your own, relying on your own insight and convictions to guide you, you can't help standing out."

"Surely standing out would increase your chances for advancement," said A.

"Come on. Standing out earns you a black mark in and of itself. It incites envy: the 'who-does-he-think-he-is' syndrome. Someone once summed it up this way: 'The greatest task of a bureaucrat is to survive without having his feet pulled out from under him by someone else.' It's no exaggeration to say this is what's uppermost in the minds of Japanese bureaucrats."

Never Find Fault with Your Seniors

"Are there any other characteristics of the species I should know about?" A asked.

"Let's see. They never find fault with the work of their seniors. In general, any departure from previous procedure or policy—an implied criticism of what your predecessors have done—is bad news. It goes against one of the most important of all the unwritten laws. That is why most administrative officials seeking to rise in the world are extremely conservative and rely heavily on precedent."

"Then nothing new can ever be done," he replied.

"You'll understand after you've lived in this country a while longer. When bureaucrats do implement a new policy, it is because, somewhere in the background, the media or special interest groups are yelling and screaming their dissatisfaction with the status quo. When the Diet members add their voices, enlarging the debate, then and only then do the bureaucrats stir themselves to action."

"Reluctantly, you mean?"

"In many cases, yes. But when you implement a new policy under those circumstances, people will realize you have no intention of wounding your superiors. If the new policy fails, you can always shrug off blame, so the bureaucrats are at ease. That's why, you see, the principle of 'Do no work' is so important. A consummately skillful bureaucrat, however, will manipulate the media, pressure groups, and Diet members when he wants to break a precedent."

"Japanese bureaucrats have their wily side too, don't they?"

"Ones like that are few and far between, though. And they can't pull it off without exquisite timing."

"If a private organization was staffed with people like that, it would go under."

"This is the national government we're talking about; the government bureaucracy will never fall apart. That could only happen if Japan ceased to exist as a nation."

"True," he said. "Knowing that the place you work for will never go belly-up would give you a terrific feeling of security, wouldn't it. And yet there's something I don't quite understand: with an unshakable foundation beneath you like that, a person ought to be able to take significant risks. According to you, though, bureaucrats are anything but adventuresome."

"That's because, as I said before, they are evaluated on a demerit system. As long as bureaucrats get points off for slip-ups, daring behavior can only work against them. If they would ever change the rating system, though, you'd see a tremendous release of power."

"On the other hand, Japan Inc. has enough power as it is to keep the world in awe, so maybe they should just leave well enough alone!"

"The power of Japan Inc.," I said, "may owe something to the abilities of its bureaucrats, but the real reason for the country's economic development lies in the support of the people, who sacrifice their own comfort for the sake of Japan Inc. If the people of Japan rose up tomorrow and refused to make any more sacrifices, this country could never maintain its present might."

"In other words, you're saying it's better for Japan's prosperity to maintain the spirit of sacrifice and not upset the status quo."

"Yes, if we stick to the three great principles. But the spirit of self-sacrifice for the greater good has built-in limitations. If we pursue still greater prosperity down the same road, we only end up creating discord. The EU and the Asian nations, not to mention your own country, are all urging us to do something about our chronic trade imbalance. The only solution is for us to end the demerit system and do more to bring out people's individual abilities, the way it's done in the United States. Then, even without a spirit of universal self-sacrifice, we could easily maintain our competitiveness as a nation. The pity is that so many people don't understand something so simple."

The Pleasure of Pain

"Still, I wonder why bureaucrats are so conservative," A reflected. "There's got to be more to it."

"I won't say this applies to everybody," I answered, "but for people in management positions, the peculiarities of their life cycle also work to push them toward conservatism. The typical age of retirement from a ministry is fifty to fifty-five. So after age fifty, as a government official faces the imminent end of his career, he naturally begins to think about the cushy job he'll get in the private sector after retirement. After years of giving everything to his job, always putting the needs of the organization before his own happiness, now all he wants to do is finish up without making any serious errors so that he can land a soft job in some famous public corporation or in private industry. Government pensions are low; as his compensation for years of self-effacement in the bureaucracy, he moves on in order to collect a fat retirement fee elsewhere. But if he muffs his job at the end, he gets nothing. It's like a game of Parcheesi, where just as you're about to make it home, you get sent back to the starting line. Nobody wants that."

"I know what you're saying," said A, "but basically, it's the job of an administrator to take risks; someone whose motto is 'Safety First' doesn't deserve a high salary."

"Think of it this way. Their high salaries are a reward for having sacrificed their personal lives for the sake of Japan, Inc. That ought to lessen the irritation."

"How about paying people according to their ability? Doesn't that ever happen?"

"No," I replied, "it doesn't work the way it does in the States. It's all based on seniority. If for some reason it becomes necessary to evaluate people, you look at how willing they've been to sacrifice themselves for the organization, or at how little trouble they have caused. The quickest way to do that is to see how faithfully they live by the three great principles."

"I could never cut it," A said.

"Of course you couldn't. The only way to cut it is to become a total masochist."

"What makes you say that?"

"Think about it. You have to come to work before everyone else even though you have nothing to do, and stay late if a colleague works overtime, just to keep him company. You come to work even when you're sick, unless you're at death's door. Then and only then do you allow yourself to use your paid vacation time. All you're doing is shortening your own life by relinquishing your individual rights. In Japan, people are expected to suffer at their jobs and to turn that into pleasure. A good worker is one who can successfully carry out this inversion, or perversion, of normal responses."

"'Perversion'? That's a pretty harsh word."

"The classic example is an event carried out in Japan in midsummer and midwinter, known as a *gaman taikai*, or endurance test. In summer, when the temperature is up in the nineties, you put on a heavy padded jacket and sit by a hibachi with a hot fire going, repeating over and over, 'How cool I am, how cool I am!' In winter it's just the reverse: you soak in ice-cold water and tell yourself you're not cold at all. Self-flagellation is seen as a form of self-discipline and purification—there's even a saying, *shinto mekkyaku sureba hi mo mata suzushi*: 'Clear your mind of mundane thoughts, and you will find even fire cool.' So self-flagellation becomes a praiseworthy act."

"Run that saying by me once more?"

"'Clear your mind of mundane thoughts, and you will find even fire cool.' It was spoken by a medieval Zen monk named Kaisen, when he and over a hundred other monks were roasted alive in their temple by warlord Oda Nobunaga. The idea is that if you concentrate all your mental powers and attain a mental state of perfect serenity, free from all ideas and thoughts, your senses will also fade away until you could be burned alive and feel nothing. The power of the mind enables you to withstand all pain."

"But that's crazy," A exclaimed. "Fire is hot, and pain hurts: those are facts, man."

"Even in the West, you have Christ, who was crucified, as the central figure in your scheme of values. Or there's Joan of Arc, who was burned at the stake. In fact, Western saints all died painful deaths. The perversion of pain into pleasure can be seen everywhere."

"No, no, that's completely different. Christ sacrificed himself out of love for his tormentors. He's a figure of mercy and compassion. The same can hardly be said for Japanese bureaucrats, if they're motivated only by their dreams of advancing their careers. In other words, people in Japan sacrifice themselves out of self-love. In the West, self-sacrifice is rooted in altruism."

"I see what you mean. We have another saying in Japanese, *tenjo tenga yuiga dokuson*: 'In Heaven and in Earth, only I am lord.' This is supposed to represent the state of enlightenment. It certainly is a far cry from 'Love thy neighbor.'"

"In the West," A said, "acts of self-affliction are a sign of mental instability. No sane person would inflict injury on himself."

"I agree with you there," I said, adding "maybe partly because I spent such a long time in the United States myself. That's exactly why I used a term like 'perversion' to begin with."

"I'd rather not work at all than suffer while I worked. There's no way suffering would ever change to pleasure. Any philosophy that says it does is only encouraging people to escape reality and lose themselves in a world of perverted, upside-down values."

"Here's where a lot of Japanese would say, 'There! That just goes to show you, a foreigner can never understand the Japanese mind.' In that sense, I guess the Japanese are unique. And lots of them are in love with their own uniqueness."

Working Up a Sweat

"What I've come to see since getting back to Japan," I said, "is that actions that only a deranged person would undertake overseas are taken here by otherwise perfectly sane and normal individuals. So it doesn't really work to measure Japan by the standards of the West."

"That argument leads straight to the idea that Japanese are different from everybody else. I believe that Americans and Japanese are born exactly the same. Look at Japanese-Americans in the United States, for one thing. They certainly aren't into self-sacrifice the way Japanese people are."

"In Japan there is a strong belief that if you just have the right attitude, you can bear up under any adversity. People are trained from an early age to see how well they can stand up to adversity. That's why the masochistic elements of their makeup are emphasized. It's a form of idealistic stoicism."

"Now don't be offended," he cautioned, "but wasn't it precisely Japan's over-reliance on that line of thinking that led straight to defeat in World War Two?"

"Absolutely. All the more reason why I personally feel that the Japanese 'Where there's a will, there's a way' mentality has definite limits. A philosophy that glorifies self-sacrifice might have an appeal in some Arab fundamentalist states, but I know very well it would never go over in the industrialized nations of the West. After all, Japanese idealism went so far as to embrace a mass fantasy of *kamikaze*, the 'divine wind' of protection. Supposedly, the gods sent storms in the thirteenth century to repel Mongol invaders; during World War Two, the idea was revived."

"Then you agree with me that the idea that pain can become pleasurable is hogwash?"

"Yes," I replied, "carried to extremes, but what I want to get across is that for most Japanese, penance of this type is not consciously painful at all. They have an internal switch of some kind that can transform what is clearly painful and make it pleasurable. Test it for yourself. Go up to people who appear to be suffering and ask them if they are. Nine times out of ten they'll say, 'Goodness no. I love it.' "

"Weird."

"Menial physical labor is a perfect example. It's known as 'working up a sweat.' No matter how much ability a person may have, he voluntarily takes on unpopular chores to demonstrate his willingness to sacrifice himself for the group. When I first joined the Ministry of Health and Welfare, I did everything from making Xerox copies to cleaning the floor, even though I didn't actually want to."

"At least you admit you didn't want to. That's normal. Still, how bizarre! A medical doctor with a distinguished career in the States goes to work for the Japanese government making copies and cleaning floors!"

"The idea of sharing in futility with everyone else makes a kind of sense in a village-type society like the Japanese bureaucracy. Let me give an example. Suppose a certain group wants a bigger grant from the ministry. In America, a representative would write a letter setting forth the merits of his proposal, along with a recommendation from some eminent expert. Here, such methods don't pay off."

"So what do you do?"

"You go to see the man in charge again and again, even if you have nothing particular to say to him. If he's out, you leave your business card. In time, the stack of cards on his desk gets to be quite high. Sometimes the thickness of the stack determines the amount of the grant. By making repeated trips to his office, you impress upon him your sincerity as you demonstrate your willingness to sacrifice your limited, precious time. This can swing the balance in your favor when it comes time for him to make up his mind. The expression used to describe this behavior, *ohyakudo o fumu*, refers literally to an old custom of walking back and forth one hundred times in front of a shrine, repeating a prayer each time.

"From my point of view, though, visitors like this are a pain in the neck. They force you to interrupt your work and waste time in meaningless chit-chat. I suggested that we require people to make appointments, but then I was told that the real work gets done after five anyway. What can you do?"

"I don't care how many calls you make to somebody's office," A said, "in the States, if your proposal isn't worth a damn, you won't get a grant. And I can't imagine people who have attained a certain status doing copying or office cleaning just to show off their willingness to sacrifice themselves."

"I was taken aback at first too," I agreed. "But within Japanese society, this idea of 'working up a sweat' is thought to be an effective way of raising group productivity."

"Really. But productivity is also enhanced if a person of real ability demonstrates leadership; creative responses become possible, too."

"As far as creativity goes, you have a point. But there's also a strong argument to be made that a leaderless society like Japan has not only proved itself able to compete with the West on an equal footing but is actually winning the competition."

Don't Excel

"Listening to you, I can't help feeling the day may come when we'll have to sacrifice our personal lives the same way the Japanese do, just to stay competitive," said A.

"The question is," I answered, "on whose terms the competition is conducted. The flaw with the 'work up a sweat' mentality is that people caught up in it have no chance to acquire any cultural polish."

"Well, with no time of their own, and work to do around the clock, how could they?"

"Exactly. What's more, strange as it may seem, in a group situation like the bureaucracy, letting others see that you are a person of culture can sometimes work against you—and it's never to your advantage."

"Why on earth would that be?"

"A former director general once told me that he couldn't begin to count the number of times he went out of his way to avoid sounding like a man of culture. He told me I ought to be careful, too. He recommended dirty jokes as the best remedy. To get along in the world, he said, you have to talk about things that the masses can understand. It's exactly what Machiavelli wrote in *The Prince*: if you want to succeed, you mustn't show that you are more sophisticated than others. My friend just put it a little more bluntly."

"That's funny. In America, a cultured background is a powerful tool. Someone with cultural attainments has an intimate understanding of the creative process. Besides, people are all different, and if they are educated in a way to draw out their individuality, they will all develop some sort of proficiency, it seems to me. Isn't that how culture grows?"

"Japan has a different philosophy of education," I said. "The basic principle is that everyone should be alike and act alike. Reciting the company precepts in unison, staying late even though you have nothing particular to do—both are rituals by which employees promise each other to give up their individuality and sacrifice themselves for the company. You could say that the three great principles are the major tenets of Japanese egalitarianism."

"In the States, the higher up a person is in an organization, the more ability and acumen he usually has. I suppose it's rather different in the seniority system."

"You got that right. It's extremely common for people with authority to have less ability than those working under them. Working for an incompetent boss is just something you have to put up with; people praise you quite openly for doing so. Besides, the personnel bureau arranges things so you can be reassigned to another post in two years, so that it's bearable."

"Why two years?" he asked.

"For one thing, the authority of the bureaucratic structure is awesome; to prevent individuals from abusing the power it confers, strict time limits are imposed on the posts they serve. Also, because the system offers no rewards for special ability, little attention is paid to the training of specialists. Jacks-of-all-trades who can handle a variety of assignments are valued more highly. For that purpose, a maximum of two years at any one post is about right."

"So the generalist is preferred over the specialist."

"By definition, a specialist is someone who knows more about his field than others. Another reason for the policy is probably to suppress the feelings of envy such people inevitably cause," I replied.

"Of course there is envy in the United States too, but I still have trouble believing that a society has to put so much emphasis on the containment of envy. In the West, as you know, envy is considered fundamentally evil; the tenth commandment, 'Thou shalt not covet,' is part of the bedrock of the Judeo-Christian tradition. Of course that doesn't mean that people don't envy one another, but anyone who is openly envious of others becomes an object of scorn, so people go to great lengths to keep their envy under wraps. Those who can't are condemned to remain at the bottom of society.

"Besides, if you were constantly worrying about the envy of

others, you wouldn't be able to live your life according to your own beliefs. In a society that attaches importance to individual abilities, being conspicuous is pretty much unavoidable."

"If you study Japanese society through the prism of envy, a lot becomes clear," I said.

"The more I learn about Japan, the more I see how different it is from the West. Where I work, every day during lunch hour the whole company does stretching exercises together, called 'radio calisthenics.' That's something else I can't figure out."

"Don't look on them as stretching exercises. We do the same thing at 3:00 P.M. in the ministry. It's something like the chanting of the company precepts: everybody performing the activity all together has meaning in and of itself."

"After so many years of living in the United States, isn't it awfully difficult for you to readjust to the logic of the village society?" he asked.

"The peculiar logic of Japan, or of the bureaucracy, is definitely hard to accept. But I'll tell you, the incessant parry and thrust of American-style logic can be awfully tiring, too. The Japanese way of doing things is surprisingly comfortable by comparison. I have mixed feelings about it all."

"There is a certain gentleness in human relations here," he said.

"Some people believe that gentleness is the secret of Japan's current success. And a certain number of foreign countries have taken up the Japanese system, too. It's had quite an impact in America, too, hasn't it? Isn't that one reason why you're over here working for a Japanese firm in the first place?"

"Exactly. What I can't stand, though, is the nosiness hiding behind the tolerance and gentleness. That and the total disregard of the value of the individual's personal life."

"I know what you mean," I answered. "Not only that, in the bureaucratic world, there's a tendency for the philosophy of

171

tolerance to get out of hand. It ends up contributing to ineffi-ciency. For example, going to the barber during work hours, or watching television, is tolerated. Inevitably, people have to hang around till all hours to finish their work, relinquishing their private time."

"I can't get over it that a trip to the barbershop during office hours could be considered okay. That means there's no line drawn between official duties and private affairs."

"You can't be such a stickler. In a sense, even the home is an extension of the workplace, a factory for the production of industrial warriors. For all practical purposes, most Japanese men have no home. And in the ministries, the boundary between public and private is even vaguer. You could really say that a bureaucrat has no private self. That's why even if a 'pri-vate' matter like getting a haircut intrudes once a month or so, it's overlooked."

"I still can't believe there's no firm line between the home and the workplace," A mused.

"In Japanese society, your organization takes precedence over your home."

"In *Modern Times*, Charlie Chaplin issued a warning about the possibility of workers losing their individuality in modern-izing societies, as they become mere cogs in company machin-ery. Looks like Japanese society is the realization of his worst fears."

"But you see," I responded, "to the vast majority of Japanese, becoming just such a cog is the whole purpose of life."

"And their compensation is getting to go to the barber dur-ing work hours."

"Don't tell your American feminist friends this, but even though it's okay for men to go to the barbershop, women aren't allowed to go to the beauty salon."

"You're right, that's discriminatory."

"I know," I said. "It would drive some people crazy."

"My wife is always saying that Japanese women need to have their consciousness raised."

"I can understand that. I know how she feels, even though I'm a man. At the ministries, women always take a back seat. Except for the few career women, that is. They're also forced to accept the unwritten rule that they're there to wait on the men. An American woman wouldn't last one hour."

Glass Ceilings and Walls

"Are there a lot of rules that give men more leeway than women at the ministerial offices?" he asked.

"Not in so many words, no. They would never be so indiscreet, or so frank, as to come right out and say that women are prohibited from such-and-such. Instead, they'll give them special consideration by announcing that women don't have to come along on a drinking outing, or asking them where they'd like to go when everyone goes out for a meal together. That special consideration has a catch, however, because it only serves to fence off the men and the women. American career women talk about a glass ceiling that prevents them from rising to the highest levels of responsibility where they work. In Japan, you could say there is a glass ceiling and a glass wall, too. Things are set up so that in the end, women can't act together with men."

"A pretty sophisticated form of discrimination," he offered.

"None of the men even sees it as discrimination, and I'll bet a fair amount of the women don't see it that way, either."

"There are a lot of women in my company, but the men all expect them to serve them tea and snacks."

"That's right, and the ones who do are really fussed over," I said. "There's a basic assumption that women are inferior to men."

"Until about thirty years ago," said A, "sex discrimination was rampant in the United States too, so Americans are in no position to brag, but at least there's a general belief that discrimination is wrong, and there are laws against it. But in a place like the bureaucracy where the official line is so often understood to be different from usual practice, even with laws to back you up, it must be extremely hard to bring about any substantive change."

"The Japanese bureaucracy is a bastion of conservatism. In society at large, understanding of the equality of the sexes has come a long way, but you're probably right that the bureaucracy will be the last place to get rid of sex discrimination."

"In the United States," he said, "if you asked a female co-worker to get up and fix you a cup of coffee, you'd be strung up."

Vagueness and Doublethink

"But the fact that Japan doesn't see everything in black and white terms, the way America does, is one of the nice things about the country," I said. "Running around yelling about equality of the sexes will only tick people off. Japanese prefer to leave things vague. That's part of the strength and vitality of the country, and that's again why Japanese productivity is so high."

"Is watching TV on the job part of that 'vagueness'? In America you'd be fired in a second."

"I know. But in Japan, people tend to overlook such things. In that sense, you could say Japanese society is more tolerant. Even in the United States, though, don't office workers stop everything to watch a space shuttle liftoff or presidential election returns?

"Yes, but those are rare exceptions to the rule."

"At the ministries, it's okay to watch anything that's tacitly considered a national event," I explained.

"Such as?"

"Telecasts of Diet proceedings, high school baseball tournaments, grand sumo tournaments, the All-Star game, the Japan Series, the Olympics, the Asian Games, major events involving the imperial family . . . stuff like that."

"Diet proceedings I can see, but surely baseball and sumo have nothing to do with work. Aren't there always people coming and going in ministry offices? What would they say?"

"Japan's liquid crystal technology is the best in the world. If you watch a liquid crystal TV screen using a cordless earphone, who's going to know? Besides, bureaucrats have charge over national administration. They have to stay informed about whatever the nation as a whole is watching and enjoying."

"Sounds like an excuse to me," A said. "Besides, how could the whole nation all be concentrating on one event at the same time?"

"Well, think of football in the States."

"Lots of people hate it."

"In Japan, whatever is deemed 'national' excites universal interest. Golf and karaoke are the same. Once the group approves, everybody falls into line."

"Weird. Now that you mention it, though, I can think of lots of examples," said A.

"Right? Being the same as everybody else is very important for getting along in Japanese society."

"What about people who just can't get excited about something?" A asked.

"The group logic is invincible, so that hardly ever happens. But when it does, those people often just talk themselves into liking whatever it is. People with a knack for doing that will go far in Japan."

"But that's horrible. It means living a lie."

"Japanese people are used to making a clear distinction between *honne*, or real feelings, and *tatemae*, or the face they put on things, so there's no internal conflict. In fact, to take it a step further, the ability to juggle *honne* and *tatemae* without conflict is considered the mark of a true adult. That's why people like me who go around saying what they really think all the time are ridiculed as big babies. Here lies the biggest difference between the United States and Japan," I said.

"George Orwell wrote a scathing criticism of totalitarian society in his book *1984*. One of his main points is that something called 'doublethink' is necessary to support totalitarianism. Doublethink is defined as the ability of a mind to hold two mutually contradictory ideas, and accept them both. Sounds like a perfect description of how Japanese accommodate *honne* and *tatemae*. I'm afraid if a fascist power wanted to lead the Japanese in a certain direction, it would be all too easy to manipulate their intelligence.

"Just think of the events of World War Two. Ever since then, the Japanese have been suspicious of political authority, but they might well still be capable of being marched off in some direction against their will."

What Happens
to Violators
of the Code

Invitation from the French Chargé d'Affaires

On the morning of July 21, 1992, I found a fax on my desk at work. It was an invitation from the French chargé d'affaires to attend a dinner reception at the French Embassy in honor of the visit to Japan of Michel Rocard.

I couldn't figure it out; the only Michel Rocard I knew of was the former premier of France. Naturally I had never met him, nor did my work at the quarantine office have any connection with France. So why the sudden invitation to such a famous man's reception?

Puzzled, I telephoned the embassy. The woman who took my

call greeted me by name and inquired if they would have the honor of my attendance. Clearly she had been expecting my call. Still vaguely nonplussed, I told her I would be there and hung up.

It still seemed hard to believe. What possible connection could there be between me and this man who represented his country to the world? Perhaps it was somehow the doing of a friend in the Foreign Ministry; I gave him a call, but he too had no explanation.

"As long as you've been invited, why not just go, without worrying too much about it?" he said casually. He himself frequently attended conferences and dinner receptions for world leaders in connection with his job, so it was easy for him to say. "It's surely not a mistake. Hey, I know, I'll bet it has something to do with your statements to the media these days." Then he added, "Don't forget, Rocard has been the French premier, and he's a leading presidential contender as well, so when you talk to him you should call him 'Premier.' That's standard protocol." I became even more nervous. After all, I had never even met the Japanese prime minister nor set foot in any ambassador's official residence.

Inner Secrets of the Bureaucracy

After two or three days, still unsure of myself, I placed another call to the French Embassy and asked to speak to whoever was in charge of planning the soiree. A second secretary took the line in the chargé d'affaires' stead. I explained who I was and asked if I would have a chance to speak directly to the chargé d'affaires and the guest of honor at the party.

"Certainly. It's a small, informal gathering of only some thirty or so; you should have ample time to speak with both of them."

"But I can't speak French."

"Don't worry. Everyone in the embassy, including Premier Rocard, can speak English." Sure enough, he had called him "Premier."

"May I ask why I've been invited? I'd like to know before meeting the premier."

"You contributed an article to the *Japan Times* the other day, didn't you, Monsieur Miyamoto? The chargé d'affaires was very interested in what you wrote."

At last I understood. Yes, the July 20 Opinion page of the paper had just run an essay of mine entitled "Time to Stress Individualism."

The article dealt mainly with the question of vacations. I had written about the intractability of the Japanese bureaucracy on the matter of vacations, based on my own experiences as I had described in my first article for the *Monthly Asahi*.

I had also said this: "Once Japan decides to become a member of Western society, it is important that its people embrace Western values. It is absurd to produce high-quality products when your living standard lags far behind.

"The life philosophy that views work as a tool to enrich one's personal life is far more humane than a philosophy that sacrifices one's personal life for the sake of the organization. When the Japanese prime minister emphasizes the importance of Japan becoming a 'superpower of high living standards,' he should stress the importance of individualism and downgrade the outdated philosophy of self-sacrifice." This idea had apparently attracted the attention of the French chargé d'affaires; my invitation had been no fluke.

"I'm delighted to hear that. Now, the invitation says nothing about what to wear. Would an ordinary business suit be appropriate?"

"Certainly."

"May I ask what other Japanese will be there?"

"The Japanese guest of honor will be Finance Minister Hata.

From the Foreign Ministry, we expect the Vice-Minister of Political Affairs, Monsieur Koji Kakizawa. There will also be various Diet members with close ties to France, as well as private citizens."

After hanging up, I found myself equally amazed at the speed of my invitation as I was at the fact of the invitation itself. The article in question had appeared on July 20; my fax invitation had been on my desk promptly the following morning. The embassy was part of the government administration; I couldn't help marveling at the swiftness of this response, which was unthinkable for Japan.

Having sometimes been in the position of choosing guests for a dinner party for the Minister of Health and Welfare, I can say that the selection process involves an unbelievable number of meetings and an incredible waste of time. Final approval for the guest list rests with a special panel, and just drafting a tentative plan takes four or five days. Another four or five days are necessary for behind-the-scenes negotiations in order to win the approval of each division. Generally at this stage, people chosen by younger bureaucrats as "likely to prove entertaining" are eliminated.

An investigation is then made into the accomplishments, alma maters, and reputations of each of the projected guests, and any with potential minus factors are summarily eliminated. Of particular importance at this stage is the question of status. Someone who has been in the news but lacks the requisite status doesn't stand a chance. Someone like me, needless to say, would never even be considered.

The question of status is interwoven in the bureaucrat's philosophy of life. A senior friend of mine in the ministry explained the inner secrets of the bureaucracy to me this way:

"Miyamoto, all sorts of people will come to you and pay you respect. But you mustn't think it's because you're important. People are bowing to your position. They have no particular respect for you as an individual at all. Unfortunately, some people seem to lose sight of that distinction. I don't want that to happen to you."

This comment expresses a general truth, but at the same time it shows clearly the importance of "self-abnegation" in the bureaucracy, where your job comes first. Whoever can best perform his assigned role (*yaku*) in the bureaucracy is the best bureaucrat (*yakunin*). Status is also conferred on bureaucrats according to their work. In fact, as long as the guests at a dinner party for the ambassador or a high-level official have sufficiently high status, anyone at all would do.

Moreover, because most bureaucrats worry above all about protecting their own hides, anyone even faintly questionable would never make it to the guest list. Safer by far to concentrate on achieving an appropriate balance in status among the guests.

And so the guest list takes gradual shape, with all those hurdles to be crossed. With Japanese bureaucrats in charge of planning, an occasion on the scale of the dinner reception for Premier Rocard would require at least one month to finalize the list of invitees.

Marveling over the vast apparent difference in bureaucratic procedure between France and Japan, I thought of the opening ceremony of the Barcelona Olympic Games, when the Olympic flame was lit by shooting an arrow from a huge distance. In Japan, such a feat would never have been tried. During planning sessions, someone would have been sure to say, "What if he misses?" Given the emphasis in this country on safety and unanimity, dissenting voices will always succeed in quashing any bold, inventive ideas.

Discrimination and Blind Equality

I realized there was one more little problem to be cleared before I could attend the affair. The invitation read "Madame et Monsieur." Of course I could simply have gone alone, but I decided to invite my female companion. I could well imagine how her eyes would shine when she heard the news. No one else in the Ministry of Health and Welfare knew of her existence. But I decided to take her along on this occasion, knowing it would mean an end to my little secret.

Why keep it a secret, you may ask. When I was living in New York, an acquaintance in the Finance Ministry had given me this advice: "If you're going back to Japan to work in a government office, don't ever tell them you're with a *gaijin* (foreigner). The Ministry of Foreign Affairs would be one thing, but a place like the Ministry of Health and Welfare is extremely conservative. If you have any hope of succeeding there, keep it under your hat."

As a result, unfair as it seemed, I had asked her to be patient for a while before I let people know about our relationship. That I had made the right decision soon became eminently clear, as my colleagues began probing curiously about my romantic involvements in America. In the end, to a man they said things like, "Lucky for you you're not saddled with a *gaijin*. Then your kids would be of mixed blood. There'd be nothing for them to do but go into the entertainment business." Hearing these same people voice pious platitudes about the evil of racial discrimination, I would shake my head all over again at the convenience of *tatemae* and *honne*.

Once I'd established myself as an "eligible bachelor," however, I found people wouldn't let well enough alone. They offered to set up *miai* for me, official introductions to prospective marriage partners. Since I couldn't exactly offend them with a flat refusal, I racked my brains for a diplomatic way out. Sometimes someone would set up a *miai* without consulting me. When I expressed unwillingness, I would be told, "Now, don't be that way about it. You've got to at least meet her, or I'll lose face." It finally dawned on me that they weren't really concerned about my future, despite their assurances that this was the case; in fact, they were motivated by a desire to secure their own futures.

In the midst of this deluge of kind offers, I learned something very interesting. As a man, people advised me to hurry up and settle down; "get married, start a family," I was told over and over. No one spoke up for my rights as an individual to live the way I chose. Surely there are many paths in life, and what counts is that we have the tolerance to respect others' life choices made out of sincere convictions, whether we agree with them or not. But the message I got was clear: "Go along with what the group thinks is best." The pressure to conform left no room for individual freedom.

The Japanese seniority system makes it easy for people to try to force their values on junior colleagues. They believe unquestioningly in the primacy of vertical relationships. Bowing to the judgment of a senior in work-related matters may make sense, but they apply pressure even in personal areas of life. Tremendous energy is required to slough off that pressure and live according to your convictions.

The bureaucracy may have "blind equality," but it lacks the concept of equality based on recognition of individual abilities. The Japanese bureaucracy could learn a few things from the French tricolor flag, which represents the concepts of liberty, equality, and fraternity.

Deciding to take my companion to the party, I braced myself for the inevitable fallout that would come. No longer would I be troubled by eager would-be matchmakers, but I would surely be in for even more cold and curious stares than before.

The Restrained Murmur of Conversation

The party began at 7:30 P.M. Sure enough, it was small and informal, with ample opportunity to talk to the other guests.

183

During aperitifs, the conversation was a swirl of French, English and Japanese, the atmosphere festive and heady. Unaccustomed as I was to such occasions, I found my nervousness assuaged by a little alcohol.

Premier and Mrs. Rocard appeared around eight. During the meal, I realized something unusual about the murmur of conversation in the room compared with the sort of banquet I was accustomed to attending in Japan. To make a musical analogy, it progressed like a piece of classical music from a prelude to a finale, beginning *piano* and swelling to *forte*, increasing in range as people drank more wine. And yet, although there was a generous supply of red wine, white wine, and champagne at hand, the murmur maintained a certain discreet restraint to the end.

At a Japanese banquet, by contrast, the conversation follows two distinct patterns. One is the raucous sound of unrestrained, drunken revelry; off-key, free-wheeling and dissonant. The other, which accompanies formal a *kaiseki* dinner, a type of traditional Japanese cuisine, is more like the gentle, unobtrusive sound of *koto* music, never leaving the same quiet, narrowly defined range.

During the lulls in conversation, I wondered about the difference and decided it lay in the different ways in which Westerners and Japanese control their impulses. Alcohol has the natural effect of relaxing people and making them more talkative. Feelings normally kept under wraps come to the fore, facilitating self-revelation and seduction alike as the alcohol removes inhibitions kept normally in place by the rational part of the mind.

In daily life, people are bound by morals, rules, and laws that inhibit their desires and emotions. Alcohol cuts these bonds and sets the individual free. Yet there is a difference in the process by which Westerners and Japanese use alcohol to release their feelings. The Western way is to do so gradually, with a liberal sprinkling of wit and humor. The Japanese way is either to hang on to your dignity to the bitter end, revealing nothing of your interior self, or to let yourself go all at once, indulging in "shameless" behavior. The background noise of party conversation reflects the difference in style.

Westerners control their impulses according to the occasion, allowing them gradually to surface, but never too far; when they sense themselves approaching the limit, they seek instinctively to regain control.

Japanese take a different approach, using the device of *tatemae* to hold their emotions in check most of the time. Alcohol, however, causes their controls to evaporate, releasing pent-up emotions with explosive force. Regaining control is no easy matter. You might say that the controllable limits on Japanese behavior are narrower for Japanese than for Westerners.

Unlike the Japanese who smile vaguely, unable to say no, Westerners differentiate clearly between "yes" and "no." Japanese conversation values sentimentalism over logic, while in the West, the reverse is true. It is apparent which approach permits greater objectivity.

Playing Catch with the Ball of Emotions

The game of catch provides a good metaphor for a comparison of feelings and impulses. Westerners are adept players of the game; even when alcohol increases the strength of their throw, they maintain enough control to catch the ball firmly in their glove. Early training in techniques of debate is one reason for their success.

The ability to control feelings and impulses is also strongly rooted in the early relationship of the child with its mother. In the West, separation from the mother is encouraged at an early age. Therefore, by the time adulthood is reached, people are able to manage and control even fairly strong feelings and impulses. Of course, the Western-style husband-wife relationship also contributes greatly to the ability to maintain that control. The husband and wife form a unit, and children are treated as separate individuals; most people are aware from childhood of the need to function on their own. As children move on to junior and senior high school, the parents' desire for them to quickly become independent intensifies. This is one reason why so many American children are able to pay their own way through college, despite high tuition costs. Indeed, separation from the mother shows itself in a variety of forms in daily life.

In Japan, by contrast, the family has always centered around the child. The mother-child bond is stronger than the husband-wife bond. Moreover, rather than urge the child to become independent, parents often give priority to their desire to be protective. As a result, children develop extremely dependent personalities and feel insecure about being on their own. This trend of increased dependency has recently grown even more pronounced. The mother treats her husband like a piece of huge, useless trash (*sodai gomi)* and pours love on her children exclusively. Moreover, as the children grow older, she looks on their successes as her own, viewing them as extensions of herself. For many, the mother-child bond only deepens over time.

People raised in such an environment are shy with strangers and unable to clearly articulate their own opinions. When they drink alcohol in quantity they lose control and get hit by the ball they are unable to catch. Getting hit is painful, and unpleasant, so in Japan the game of debate is shunned from the start. Consequently, two styles of conversation at dinner parties emerge: the rowdy banquet style, where people cut loose and give free rein to their emotions, and the formal style with almost no emotional display, as if a sign were up: "No Ball-playing Allowed."

"Liberated" Women

The Japanese banquets I have attended were all-male affairs where the topic of work dominated the conversation. When the alcohol begins to flow, people begin to air their grievances and to tell off-color stories. My greatest pleasure on such occasions is to keep an eye on the clock and calculate the remaining time before I can leave.

The embassy dinner was altogether different. Men and women were seated side by side, husbands and wives separated. I found myself seated between two women I had never met before. Still, conversation flowed freely. What's more, to my surprise, the Japanese women in attendance were refreshingly outspoken and candid in their views.

The lawyer's wife to my left glanced at my business card with a look of puzzlement and wondered aloud what relation a quarantine director might have with France. When I explained, she said, "How very interesting! Dr. Miyamoto, you must not give up your job." She was possessed of vivaciousness and charm. I remember being most favorably impressed.

Something that my French teacher had once said came back to me. "After they marry, Japanese women forget they are women, and before they marry, they don't let people see that they are women. But a Frenchwoman is aware of being a woman even in her seventies." That evening, however, his words didn't apply to any of the Japanese women in attendance at the party.

When men and women gather as couples, able to forget for a while that they are mommies and daddies, the dinner table sparkles. Mme. Mitterand once said, "Before I was the president's wife, I was a free woman." If Japan would offer women a level playing field and freedom to participate, society itself would sparkle. Young women of today are better educated and more assured than ever before. They refer to the young men who swarm around them with cavalier names like Asshii-kun and Messhii-kun: literally, Mr. Legs and Mr. Meals. The one means a suitor with wheels, the other, one who provides escort to fine restaurants. These hapless young men are looking not for a feminine, witty companion but for the traditional "good wife and wise mother"—a woman who will devote herself to them.

But why should such a meek creature receive such royal treatment during courtship? The answer lies in men's subconscious distrust of women. Men try to compensate for their own inner weaknesses with a strong, motherly woman. As long as that is how the majority views women, women can never advance far in Japanese society.

Premier Rocard's Toast

Around 10:30 P.M., champagne glasses were filled, and Premier Rocard and Finance Minister Hata each said a few words. When that was over, the dining room was transformed to a salon, and people milled around engaged in conversation, sipping after-dinner drinks.

The French chargé d'affaires wove among his guests, introducing each one to Premier Michel Rocard. When my turn came, he explained why I had come; I then shook hands with the premier, and said in a mixture of English and poor French, "I've had a wonderful time this evening. I hope your stay in Japan will be a fruitful one. I understand this is your wife's first visit here, and I hope it will be a pleasant and memorable occasion for her."

Then to my surprise, he encouraged me, in English, as follows: "I read your article in the *Japan Times*, too. It was very interesting. Your way of thinking is sure to spread in Japan. It's not easy to change the way people think, but don't give up."

Not only the French chargé d'affaires, but the man who

might soon occupy the most powerful position in France, had read my article and appreciated it. I was deeply honored. Even Mrs. Rocard spoke up and said she had read it too: "It must have taken great courage for you to be so honest. You are in the minority, I'm sure, but it's very important for each one to stand up for his beliefs."

"As a matter of fact," added the chargé d'affaires, "Mrs. Rocard is a psychoanalyst." He also filled her in on my past teaching position at Cornell University. Thanks to him, I was able to have an exchange of opinions with her about the structure of the Japanese psyche, the cultural background that gives rise to it, and so on. We even found we had mutual friends in New York.

Listening to Premier and Mrs. Rocard, I began to see why I'd been invited. They understood, and sympathized with, my idea that the nation owed its existence to the individual, and not the other way around. The individual is not simply a cog in the wheel of the state. They had apparently seen a similarity between my attitude in writing the article to begin with and the French love of independence.

The Nail that Sticks Out . . . Gets Pulled

After I began writing the *Monthly Asahi* articles in May 1992, all sorts of unexpected things began happening. On July 3, I went on the NHK morning TV show "Lifestyle Journal," and from August 3 to 7 I was a guest every day on a Radio Japan special program. From then on, I received a variety of media attention. The *Asahi Shimbun* even quoted my opinion in their well-known front-page column, "Vox Populi, Vox Dei."

As part of the hoopla, the *Japan Times* asked me to write an article for them, which turned out to appeal to foreigners seeking to understand Japan. There was even a response from the Italian embassy. I am grateful for the favorable attention I've drawn, but I also feel a little overwhelmed at the magnitude of my responsibility.

But back at the Ministry of Health and Welfare, naturally, I am still an "*enfant terrible.*" A colleague who joined the ministry when I did warned, "Don't tell anyone I told you this, but what they're saying now is that so many people have liked what you wrote that for now, they'll let it go, but that early next year they'll get you to resign."

Among the ordinary staff at the ministry, copies of my article were being xeroxed and passed around, and everybody was getting a kick out of them, my friend said. But since people were afraid of being found out, the xeroxing was done not on the premises but in a nearby stationery store, and then the copies were circulated secretly. The melodrama of it all was laughable. If only they'd skipped the xeroxing, bought a copy of the magazine, and read my article openly at work, my standing with the editors would have shot up!

In one of my articles I wrote that "the nail that sticks too far out can't be pounded down." But a concerned reader responded this way:

"Dr. Miyamoto, you said that a nail that sticks too far out can't be pounded down, but you should know that bureaucrats immersed in the philosophy of self-sacrifice for the organization look on criticism with a jaundiced eye. They are not to be trifled with. And they may well decide that a nail like you should be pulled out. Please, be careful."

To make sure I'm not pulled out and tossed aside like an unwanted peg, I shall do my best to grow into a big tree, roots firmly planted in the ground.

Afterword

To the casual reader, this book may seem like an exposé designed to appeal to the voyeur within us all. In fact, I have sought to use my knowledge of social psychology and the techniques of psychoanalysis to offer an analysis of group psychology in the Japanese bureaucracy and some of the problems it causes. I have written frankly about various episodes because I felt that the problems of groupism that affect all of Japan could be most clearly expressed this way. I also thought I could I elicit greater sympathy this way.

My detailed accounts of exchanges with ministry officials may create the mistaken impression that I took notes during the exchanges or taped them secretly. No such thing is true.

Psychoanalysis is the science of analyzing the human heart, similar to the analysis of a written text. It requires long training and an accumulation of much knowledge. Learning to remember objectively what the other person said, and in what context—without mixing in your own emotions—is vital.

When I first began to study psychoanalysis at Cornell Medical College, I would write down every word spoken by a patient, add my comments, and show it to my advisor. He told me, "Don't write down what the patient says. Commit it to memory. If you're going to take notes as you provide counseling, I can't instruct you."

My English was not yet fluent then, so I panicked. But my

advisor continued, "Write down the content of your exchanges with patients after the session is over. It's only forty minutes or so of talk. If you can't remember what you both said during that time, you're not qualified to be a psychoanalyst."

In Japanese, maybe I could pull it off—but in English? I didn't know what to do. He read the look on my face and encouraged me.

"I'm not saying you have to memorize every word that passes between you, verbatim. Just get down the main points. Don't forget, many of the finest psychoanalysts in America are foreigners. When they first came here, they couldn't speak the language well either. But their lack of fluency helped them to concentrate on writing down the gist of the patients' talk. Sometimes what seems like a handicap can work for you, not against you. I myself grew up speaking nothing but Hebrew. You can do it."

As a result of his encouragement, I learned the ropes and became able to remain objective as I psychoanalyzed a patient. Certainly I never expected my previous training to serve me in such good stead after joining the Ministry of Health and Welfare. But the techniques of psychoanalysis, which I spent more than a decade acquiring, are such a part of me now that I can't easily lay them aside. The vertical relationships in the Japanese bureaucracy, moreover, provide an ideal context for carrying out psychoanalysis effortlessly. Those who are low on the totem pole are expected to listen silently to their superiors and not inject their own opinions into a discussion. This, of course, is exactly what happens during a counseling session. And so I found myself beginning, naturally, to psychoanalyze my superiors. Had we been able to talk as equals, I would not have been able to do it so easily—but in the ministries, permission to speak on equal terms is rarely granted.

To ministry officials, my approach was apparently hard to take. In the first place, they must have had no idea that I was mentally recording everything they had to say, or they wouldn't have spoken as freely as they did. One official no doubt voiced the frustrations of all when he complained, "Now every time we talk to Miyamoto, we have to tell him everything we say is off the record. It's like having a damned newspaper reporter on the staff!"

To ministry officials, emotions steeped in old-fashioned sentimentality (*giri*, or obligation; *ninjo*, or human feeling; *jingi*, or benevolence and righteousness) are all-important. This shared mentality creates a strong sense of unity and security. Being dealt with in a hard-nosed, no-nonsense manner conveys to them the unwelcome message that "you and I are separate individuals"—a direct violation of the bureaucratic code of oneness. That's why officials take umbrage at my style.

In fact, indulging in the sentimental notion that we are all one leads to great problems: even if something strikes people as questionable or wrong, the group code prevents them from speaking their mind.

Virtually everyone in Japan has to live in some form of communal organization. Apparently there were a lot of frustrated people in the ministry who sensed something amiss yet felt powerless to say so. That would explain why the articles I wrote generated such an overwhelmingly positive response. The majority of letters I received essentially said: "Thanks for writing what you did. I knew something wasn't right, but I couldn't say anything. Please go on analyzing what's wrong with Japanese society."

The more I realized the existence of a silent majority of people who "know something isn't right" yet cannot bring themselves to speak out, the more convinced I am of the need to do whatever I can, however little it may be, to change Japanese society. That conviction is what prompted me to continue writing the series of articles.

The letters of support I received share another theme in common: concern for my well-being. Many readers wondered if I was wise to be so blunt. The high frequency of such responses suggests to me widespread awareness of the closed nature of Japanese society.

Ken'ichi Miyata, my editor at the *Monthly Asahi*, told me, "What you've written about life in the bureaucracy is shocking. Not just the content, but the fact that we would publicize it, makes people in today's Japan sit up and take notice—and worry on your behalf. You've broken a taboo by writing about something that everybody knows about but no one talks about. Everybody knows the situation is bad, but no one sets out to change it—maybe because they're afraid to witness the collapse of everything they've ever believed in."

It is hardly my intent to destroy everything that people have ever believed in. I must say, though, that as long as people in Japan willingly accept restraints on freedom of speech in order to prevent the collapse of what they believe in, true democracy can never take root here.

Around May 1992, when the first article appeared, pressure from the Ministry of Health and Welfare was so intense that I spent some time holed up at home, overwhelmed by mental pressure and nursing a cold. Looking back, I can only say that the denial of freedom of speech is a harsh reality in the closed-off world of the Japanese bureaucracy.

In my writings I did no more than simply state the facts of my experience and add a few words of comment. But because in so doing I violated the unwritten code of the bureaucracy, I was looked on as a heretic and subjected to scathing criticism for leaking to the outside world things that were tacitly understood never to be spoken of or revealed.

Initial response was so negative, and so intense, that my future as a bureaucrat—let alone the future of the series—was in strong doubt (the status of my career, I might add, is still up in the air). Kiyoshi Nagae, associate editor at the *Monthly Asahi*, then phoned me to say this:

"Dr. Miyamoto, you've passed the point of no return. You can never go back to your former relationship with the ministry. Your readers are looking forward to hearing what you have to say, though, and we hope you will go on writing."

That phone call gave me the mettle to withstand the pressure at work and continue writing. Without the support of Ken'ichi Miyata, I could never have brought the series to a successful conclusion. He worried over my standing with the ministry, comforted me over the telephone, and generally looked after me in a way I could never have managed without. Once again, I would like to express my thanks.

What I still can't get over today is the inability of government officials to realize that even if the masochistic, self-sacrificing spirit of the bureaucracy should fall by the wayside, the organization would be safe; it would, indeed, have a sounder and a brighter future. To fear that a collapse in self-abnegation would spell the downfall of the organization is unrealistic.

Deep down, most individuals feel that they owe their continued existence to the organization: if that larger community disintegrates, they fear that they themselves may disappear as well. This is mass hysteria, rising out of lives spent steeped in the ethic of the group. From my treatment of patients suffering from such hysteria, I know that, upon recovery, they realize how silly and laughable their fears were.

Returning a patient suffering from mass hysteria to normal is easy. It requires only that the patient adopt a way of life in which individual needs come first. Each person should be allowed to exercise common sense in daily life—and can willingly do so, given the chance. This also means adopting values that are in tune with the times.

Then, just as in other countries, people here can enjoy the knowledge that their lives are rich and full, without having to be sacrificed for the good of the company, and that society will become more livable for all. Moreover, once the spell of mass hysteria is broken, people can indeed learn to say no to one another—thus becoming, in the eyes of the world, full adults.

The sorts of problems I have examined at length in these pages are rarely alluded to in the West, where they could never gain much of a foothold. Examples of foreign leaders of Japanese ancestry such as the late United States Senator S. I. Hayakawa or Peruvian President Alberto Fujimori indicate that Japanese people living abroad are fully capable of living strong, inner-directed lives, free from the poison of mass hysteria.

I trust it is clear by now that I did not write this book as an exposé. Sententious as it may sound, I believe that in the long run, what I have done is in Japan's best interest. If, however, in writing of events in my life at the ministry I have given offense to anyone or caused anyone pain, it can only be because my efforts to convey my sincerity failed. In that case I offer humble apologies.

Acknowledgments

Back when the *Monthly Asahi* series was just getting underway, I spoke with Dr. Satoru Saito of the Tokyo Mental Health Institute, an authority on alcohol-related problems in Japan. He told me that what I had to say would make an interesting book and introduced me to Shinjo Furuya, an editor at Kodansha. Mr. Furuya proved equally enthusiastic and took charge of the process of turning my articles into a book. To both of these men I am deeply grateful.

Finally, I would like to thank Yoshibumi Wakayama of the *Asahi Shimbun* editorial staff, for offering needed advice to improve my writing style, and to Sanpei Sato, for gracing the original Japanese edition of the book with his wonderfully witty cartoons.